Questioning Christian Origins

270.1

334 01355 0

First published 1982
by SCM Press Ltd
58 Bloomsbury Street, London WC1

Typeset by Gloucester Typesetting Services
and printed in Great Britain by
Richard Clay Ltd (The Chaucer Press),
Bungay

J K ELLIOTT

QUESTIONING

CHRISTIAN

ORIGINS

SCM PRESS LTD

TO CAROLYN

Contents

Preface

Since 1978 the monthly journal *History Today* has been running an occasional series of articles on various aspects of Christian origins. The interest aroused by these articles encouraged me to expand them and to present them anew. This book is the result. For permission to reproduce here material that originally appeared in *History Today* I am particularly grateful to the previous editor Peter Quennell and to the present editor Michael Crowder.

This book is aimed at both the student and the general reader who are interested in the historical basis of Christianity and the New Testament. Each chapter concludes with an index of the main biblical passages referred to in the preceding discussion to enable those who wish to use this book for group or private study to investigate the primary material for themselves. A short bibliography is also added to each chapter and it is to be hoped that those who wish to study more fully, and in some cases from a different point of view, the topics covered by the chapter, will find these reading lists helpful.

The bulk of the manuscript was typed by the secretaries in the Department of Theology at Leeds University and in particular by Miss Dorothy Raper and Mrs Hazel Walker. I gratefully acknowledge their work with warmest thanks.

Leeds   Keith Elliott
Easter 1981

Introduction

Questions concerning Jesus' life and teaching, influence and death occur to believers and unbelievers alike when they read the gospels. Questions also arise concerning the beginnings of the church and the post-Easter faith of the earliest Christians. The historian interested in the origins and growth of Christianity as well as the Christian concerned about the historical basis of his faith are both dependent on the books of the New Testament. Little of substance exists outside the biblical record of these first-century events.

Why did Jesus die? Did the resurrection happen? Who was John the Baptist? How did Christianity spread? Is the Acts of the Apostles historical? Who was Peter? Who was Paul? These and other questions are tackled in the following chapters. The book discusses the main events in Jesus' career: his birth, contact with John the Baptist, ministry and death. There then follows a discussion of the Easter narratives. In each of these discussions the emphasis is on the historical events that can be ascertained from the New Testament accounts. We are less concerned here with theological teaching or the nature of Christ's person except when such considerations aid the search for historical fact. There have been many attempts to search for the historical Jesus: this book does not attempt to reconstruct Jesus' life but merely to analyse from a critical historical viewpoint the validity of the New Testament stories and statements about him.

The second half of the book deals principally with the growth of Christianity. Taking the book of Acts and Paul's letters as the primary sources, but also using the gospels where relevant, an attempt is made to reconstruct the events leading from Jesus' death to the period covered at the end of Acts. Particular emphasis here is placed on Paul and Peter. If the evidence is unclear or ambiguous I have tried not to force an interpretation. Where I have felt able to make deductions some readers may consider that my conclusions are either too radical or too unorthodox, but it is hoped that the results can be substantiated by the evidence. Uncertainties and indecisiveness in other places may also be disturbing for those whose faith demands more confident statements such as 'this is how it was' rather than 'this could have been', 'this seems', or 'it is likely that', but if the evidence is not available conjecture is all that is possible.

In all this it is clear that the New Testament is being looked upon with some suspicion as an historical source. But this is a proper approach. The New Testament books are religious documents whose primary interest is not in historical facts for their own sake. Historical facts are there but are not always uppermost. Similarly the New Testament is biased: the motive of its writers was not to repeat events and sayings as a journal of record would, but to evoke faith in Jesus Christ as risen Lord and saviour as is expressly stated by John 20.30–31 and Luke 1.1–4.

The composition of the New Testament needs to be kept in mind. As far as the gospels are concerned the historical deeds and sayings of Jesus and his contemporaries were reinterpreted in the years following his death through the eyes of faith. These reinterpretations were then transmitted orally and later in written form among the early Christian communities throughout the mediterranean. The individual style and predilections of the four individual gospel writers determined what was included and how it was reported. The interests of these evangelists and the churches in which they developed were religious: the gospels were not written to satisfy our historical curiosity. The overriding influence behind the gospels is that of the risen Christ and although they tell of his birth, ministry and death, Jesus' career is reviewed in the light of the Easter belief of the writers. The picture of Jesus' life is not intended to be objectively historical. This book however attempts to provide that historical objectivity to the life of Jesus and the early church by working with and behind the evidence of the New Testament.

2

1 The Birth and Background of Jesus of Nazareth

The New Testament is the obvious and only sourcebook to which one must turn for information about Jesus' career; and one might perhaps assume that the books written first in the New Testament would be the fullest in detail. Surprisingly this is not so. The earliest books (Paul's letters and parts of Acts) are very sparse in their details about Jesus' ministry. Even when we turn to the gospels, the first one written, Mark, gives less information about Jesus' early life than the later gospels of Matthew and Luke. There are good reasons why this is so.

Paul, who is unlikely to have known or seen Jesus in his lifetime, quotes one or two of Jesus' sayings, but in general shows little knowledge of or interest in Jesus' career. His main concern is with the last few days of Jesus' life – the last supper, crucifixion, death, burial and resurrection. The basis for Paul's theology is that Jesus, who was killed, had been raised from the dead. This is the starting point for Paul's teaching on ultimate salvation and for his Christian hope. The ministry is irrelevant to Paul.

The early chapters in Acts contain much that is primitive, even though the composition of the book as a whole is likely to have been towards the end of the first century. These chapters include speeches that seem to have been based on traditional and probably oral material in order to picture the life of the earliest days of the Christian community. In these speeches the message is similar to Paul's, in so far as all that is taught about Jesus are the facts of his death, and the significance of the belief that he is still alive. We can but speculate whether this represents all that was ever taught to prospective converts about the newly proclaimed saviour, or whether further details about the man and his message were also preached to satisfy the curiosity of new believers.

Possibly at the very beginning, those who were being told about the significance of Jesus' death had known Jesus and had heard his teaching direct; but certainly by the time the New Testament was composed, the people for whom it was addressed were unlikely to have known the Jesus of history. This means that the vast majority of those who read the earliest books in the New Testament were expected to concentrate only on the saving-act of Jesus' death and resurrection, and on the new life this was believed to inaugurate. Only later did interest in Jesus' earlier career develop.

We can see this development within the gospels, beginning with Mark, who expands the primitive proclamation found in Paul and Acts by giving further and fuller details of how and why Jesus died, and also some information about Jesus' doings and sayings. Mark's gospel begins with Jesus appearing suddenly from Nazareth to be baptized by John the Baptist. He then starts his own ministry. Most of the book is taken up with the reasons why Jesus met his death. Mark's gospel is often said to be a passion narrative with an intro-duction. Certainly of Mark's sixteen chapters a good third is devoted to the last week in Jesus' life. Even the earlier chapters make constant reference to Jesus' controversies with Jewish groups. Regular antici-pations of his death are included. This development from the bald and primitive proclamation was entirely natural as people's curiosity in Jesus' career grew.

The next stage in the growth of interest in Jesus came when Christians grew curious about Jesus' family and background. The interest resulted in the birth narratives found in Matthew's and Luke's gospels (Luke 1–2; Matt. 1–2). The gospel of John was the last to be composed, and has no need to repeat these narratives be-cause in John's theology Jesus was pre-existent; that is, his career started at the beginning of time. Consequently, for John there was no need to tell a story of Jesus' miraculous birth: for him Jesus was son of God *ab initio*.

But even though the gospels do give us an increasing amount of detail about Jesus' ministry and background, they are not biographies. That is why so much of his early life is obscure. We may only assume that, in the period before he embarked on his own ministry, he was living in the shadow and influence of his mentor, John the Baptist. We have no information about Jesus' physical appearance. Even Jesus' age is not known for certain: Luke 3.23 says he was 30 at the beginning of his ministry; the Fourth Gospel implies he was much older: at an early stage in his ministry he is said to be 'not yet fifty' (John 8.57). The only well-documented period in Jesus' career before the ministry concerns the circumstances of his birth; but most of the details are legendary.

I

The stories of Jesus' birth came into the New Testament fairly late. The gospels of Matthew and Luke were written about AD 75–85, which means that at least seventy or eighty years had elapsed since the birth of Jesus before the event was written about. This interval alone makes one suspect that the record of the birth may be inaccurate, despite the often-made claim about the retentiveness of the oriental memory. In addition, the two accounts cannot be reconciled: both Matthew and Luke seem to be telling completely different stories. In fact, it is very unlikely that any of our traditional Christmas narratives are historical in the strict sense of the word. The birth stories were pious legends; and we may compare them with other examples in ancient literature, where we find childhood stories of great men, such as Herodotus' stories about the childhood of Cyrus, or Plutarch's stories about the young Alexander, or Philostratus' tales of Apollonius. In the biblical sphere Josephus and Philo both retail legends about Moses' childhood.

The gospels' birth stories satisfy that same sort of curiosity about the hero's background. But they do more than that. The nativity stories are primarily theological compilations, designed to make certain religious statements about Jesus. Their aim was to stress that Jesus' birth was unique and miraculous, and as such was accompanied by divine signs and portents. They also showed that Jesus was born of Davidic descent as the long-awaited Messiah. Prophecies and hymns dedicated to the Messiah are said in these stories to reach their fulfilment through Jesus. These and other theological motives are enclosed in a framework of legend and folklore. The story is told with a charming simplicity that has made it among the most popular of all religious literature; the narrative skill of both Luke and Matthew emphasizes the poignancy of their message.

One of the main aims of both authors' narratives is to state that Jesus was born in Bethlehem. In this both Matthew and Luke agree, although they do so in differing ways. The reason why the birthplace appeared so important was that the Messiah was expected to be of Davidic lineage and born in David's royal city. If Jesus was to be depicted in any sense as a kind of Messianic figure, then the gospel writers had to say that, in accord with the expectations and prophecies, Jesus was indeed born in Bethlehem. It is interesting to note that in the Fourth Gospel (John 7.41f.) it is reported that some people (probably of the author's acquaintance) doubted Jesus' claim to be the Messiah, because he was known to have come from Nazareth in the Galilee, and not from Bethlehem. We are told this caused a difference of opinion concerning Jesus' credentials. It was these doubts about Jesus' provenance that encouraged the composition of the birth narrative to try to prevent such splits. Since John's gospel was written about ten years after Luke it seems as if the Lucan, or Matthaean, infancy narratives – if, in fact they circulated in the area where John's gospel was written – were not successful, or rejected as spurious.

For the author of the Fourth Gospel, Jesus' parentage and hometown were of little importance; for him it is Jesus' heavenly origins which matter. John transcended purely historical considerations, although 6.42 and 7.27 show that Jesus' earthly family origins were a bar to belief in his heavenly origins, at least in some quarters. But for Matthew and Luke, Jesus' birthplace was of supreme significance. Both make great efforts to have Jesus born in the right place at the right time.

In Luke, the parents of Jesus live in Nazareth. So, in order to get them to Bethlehem, Luke says a census was taking place. Luke, as is characteristic of his universalist outlook, tries to establish the historicity of the event by stating who the Roman emperor and Roman governor of Syria were at the time. It is doubtful whether such a census could ever have taken place, and, if it did, whether Joseph, merely because he was supposedly of Davidic descent, had to be registered in Bethlehem. The important thing, so far as Luke was concerned, was that Jesus was born there. After the birth Jesus' parents returned to Nazareth.

Matthew's method of having Jesus born in the correct town is to imply that the father and mother were residents of Bethlehem at the time of his birth. Matthew then states that the family left Bethlehem for Egypt in order to escape from Herod's massacre of infants. After a sojourn in Egypt the family returned to Israel and settled in Nazareth, where, as in Luke's gospel, Jesus grew up. Both evangelists therefore agree that Jesus was born where the Messiah should have been born according to the prophets. They also agree that Jesus was subsequently brought up in Nazareth. That Jesus was 'Jesus of Nazareth' is one of the few undisputed facts about his life. Whatever else in the story of Jesus may be open to doubt, his Galilean background is firmly fixed in the tradition.

Another important element in the nativity stories in both gospels is that Jesus' birth was apparently divinely inspired. Jesus is depicted not only as Messiah but as Son of God. Again, both evangelists set about introducing the miraculous element in different ways. The divine inspiration for the birth is mediated – as so often in Jewish folklore – through an angel; angels were part of the essential apparatus of miracle stories. In Matthew it is to Joseph that the angel appears to state that Mary is to bear a miraculous son. In Luke Gabriel appears to Mary to say her son is to be the long-expected Messiah.

Another miraculous element in the stories is that outsiders learn of Jesus' birth through supernatural means and, as a result, acknowledge the momentous event. Matthew tells how Herod the King knew that the birth of Jesus brought into the world a rival king, whom he must destroy. This information is imparted to Joseph in a dream, another traditional piece of machinery in legends. Matthew also has the astrologers (or 'wise men') come to Bethlehem as the unwitting executors of Herod's malevolent plans. These men are guided to Jesus by another supernatural sign, a moving star. Having found Jesus and having paid homage, they are then divinely instructed (in this case 'in a dream') not to complete their duty to Herod by reporting that they had found the new King. Although the astrologers are necessary *dramatis personae* in Matthew's explanation of how and why Jesus' family left Bethlehem for Nazareth via Egypt, they also add to the supernatural element. Whatever these 'magi' were – and 'astrologers' is generally considered to be an appropriate translation – Matthew seems to be telling us, as Paul had said earlier, that the presence of Jesus in the world spelt doom to the 'spirits of this age' and to other powers, of which astrologers would be representatives.

Incidentally, the normal illustration of *three* wise men is not biblical. Later church tradition assumed there were three, presumably because Matthew says three gifts were presented. Matthew, however, is unlikely to mean that only three men were there: the significance of the royal gifts of gold, frankincense and myrrh is merely to emphasize the kingly nature of the Jesus of his gospel: for Matthew Jesus was Messiah and a King, and, as such, his status has to be acknowledged by the now diminishing astral and worldly powers.

The outsiders whom Luke chooses to find and worship the new-born Jesus are shepherds. They are said to learn of the birth in an angelic message. Luke's purpose in introducing shepherds is not merely to paint a pastoral scene; like Matthew, his aim is theological and symbolic. His fondness for outcasts, the lowly and the humble, is apparent throughout this gospel. Thus to have shepherds the first worshippers of Christ is entirely in keeping with Luke's vision of the purpose of Christianity. Perhaps also there is an allusion to Jesus being worshipped as the 'lamb of God' (as he is called in John's gospel). Another aspect of the pastoral tone of this tale is found in Luke's detail that Jesus' cradle was a feeding-trough, in which the baby is well wrapped up (as, of course, a baby would need to be if his cradle were a trough). Jesus' condition is described to the shepherds by the angel, and is another of Luke's supernatural signs. This is an aspect of the story which was elaborated by later tradition. The apocryphal gospels made use of Isaiah 1.3, which speaks of the ox and the ass at 'their master's crib'; and so they added animals to the scene. Jesus is then said to have been born in a stable. These additions, and the reason why Jesus' parents were not accommodated in the inn, became necessary details in the retelling of Luke's story, not only in medieval mystery plays but in our modern interpretations of Jesus' birth; but none has New Testament authority.

Another important miraculous ingredient in the original stories involves the belief that Jesus' birth was no mere spiritually inspired birth, such as could be claimed for many of the famous and holy,

8

including John the Baptist. The unique miracle is that Jesus' mother was said to be a virgin. Like the birth stories as a whole, this belief seems also to have entered the New Testament late. The epistles of Paul, which ante-date Matthew and Luke, speak of the incarnation but never of a virgin birth. Galatians 4.4 implies a natural birth; and Romans 1.3 makes no reference to a miraculous conception. Paul, arguing for Jesus' essential humanity, betrays no knowledge of a tradition that could have been used as a counter to his arguments. The virgin birth tradition is as unnecessary to Paul's theology as it is medically implausible. But for Luke and Matthew the virgin birth of Jesus was another way of stressing their belief in Jesus' uniqueness. We have already noted that John's gospel preserves a tradition that acquaintance with Jesus' parents was a bar to belief in his Messiah-ship; and perhaps that is one reason why Jesus' conception is described as divine.

II

Besides stressing the supernatural and miraculous elements in the nativity stories, Matthew and Luke rely heavily on their biblical and cultural heritage when they tell of the Messiah's birth. Both authors modelled their narratives on Old Testament passages. For Matthew, Jesus throughout his career fulfils Old Testament prophecy; for Luke, pre-Christian Messianic hymns are sung over the newly born Jesus.

So far as the fulfilment of Old Testament prophecy is concerned, it is well known that in some parts of the New Testament an Old Testament quotation seems to have influenced the details in the New Testament narration. Elsewhere it seems as if the New Testament authors have had difficulties in finding a suitable Old Testament quotation to match well-known facts about Jesus. Both these tend-encies seem to have been at work in the early chapters of Matthew. As examples of how an Old Testament prophecy has influenced Matthew's contents, we see that the birth in Bethlehem is said to fulfil a prophecy (Matt. 2.6); the call from Egypt is similar (2.15). The massacre of the innocents is created from a prophecy quoted out of Jeremiah (Matt. 2.17–18). As an example of the opposite tendency, we note that, at the end of Matthew's infancy story, Matthew tries to justify the reason why Jesus was an inhabitant of Nazareth. Here he quotes from an otherwise unknown prophecy, 'he shall be called a Nazarene'. Whatever the origin of this quotation, Matthew obviously felt it was a suitable 'proof text' in line with the biblical quotations.

The most famous of the Old Testament passages quoted by Matthew in his birth story comes at 1.23. Here a well-known Messianic prophecy is applied to Jesus. This is the prophecy from Isaiah 7.14 'A virgin shall conceive and bear a son and he shall be called Emmanuel'. The interesting thing about this prophecy is that it is quoted by Matthew from the Greek translation of the original Hebrew (that is, the Septuagint). In the Hebrew there is no mention of 'virgin'; the word used means 'young girl' (Hebrew has a different word for 'virgin'). The Septuagint translators, however, rendered the Hebrew by *parthenos*, which means 'virgin'. It seems likely, therefore, that the virgin birth tradition developed in Matthew's gospel – and ultimately in Christian theology – out of this mistranslation of the Hebrew Isaiah. Thus the need to fulfil this Septuagint version of the quotation encouraged Matthew to describe the uniqueness of the Messiah's birth as he did. Matthew would also have been aware that his gentile readers, familiar as they were with stories of theogamies, would have found such an element in the story of the Messiah's origins understandable.

As well as these specific biblical quotations that influenced Matthew's nativity story, another Old Testament theme permeates this gospel. Throughout it the church is shown to be the new Israel, and Jesus is seen as a new Moses. That is why it is important to Matthew to have Jesus called like Moses out of Egypt. Here the massacre of the innocents parallels Pharaoh's slaughter in Exodus, and there are other parallels between Jesus and Moses. For instance, the site of the great sermon is placed by Matthew up a mountain – in Luke, the sermon is on the plain – perhaps to echo Moses' giving of his law-code. Jesus' new law in Matthew restates many aspects of the Mosaic code; and it is significant that Matthew begins his great sermon with the Beatitudes, which parallel the Ten Commandments. Many scholars have argued that Matthew's gospel as a whole was planned to parallel the five-fold division of the so-called books of Moses in the Old Testament. Certainly when he told the birth story, Matthew had the figure of Moses very much in mind.

Luke's birth stories also seem to have been modelled on Messianic proof texts. Several of the hymns in Luke 1 and 2 were originally pre-Christian Jewish hymns of expectation for the Messiah. Some were applied by the followers of John the Baptist to John. The Christians, in telling of their Saviour's birth, appear to have taken their cue from the followers of the Baptist. Many of the details of Jesus' nativity in Luke are paralleled in the very full account of John's birth. It is unlikely that the Christians would have invented the stories about John's birth; but it was not unnatural for them to repeat these stories and then follow them by similar stories about Jesus. John's movement began before Jesus'; and so it is probable that legends about him had developed earlier.

The birth stories of Jesus were modelled on the existing stories about the Baptist in order to show that Jesus was the more significant of the two men. There are certainly parallels; but there are also details that stress Jesus' superiority. Among the parallels Luke says that the birth of both men is heralded by Gabriel, the angelic messenger. Both Mary and Zechariah (John's father) are told that their offspring will be 'great', and that the respective births will be spiritually encouraged; and both are bidden not to be afraid. Hymns are sung over each baby. It is significant that the birth of Jesus is dated from the conception of John (Luke 1.26). The two mothers are said to be related. To emphasize the supremacy of Jesus, Luke reserves the highest titles, 'Son of God', 'Son of the Most High', 'King of Israel', for Jesus. Another way of showing Jesus' preeminence is seen when the two pregnant women, Mary and Elizabeth, meet; Elizabeth's baby is said to jump in her womb in obeisance to the baby Mary is carrying, and Elizabeth addresses Mary as the 'mother of my Lord'. It is, of course, characteristic of the gospels as a whole to stress John's inferiority to Jesus and the Lucan birth stories fulfil this aim.

The process of borrowing sayings and stories that originated in John's movement, and using them for Christian purposes, is apparent even in the copying of the New Testament by later scribes. The well-known hymn 'The Magnificat', which like many of the Lucan hymns has passed into church liturgy, is ascribed in most manuscripts to Mary; and thus it appears as a hymn of praise over Jesus in Luke 1.46–55. But some manuscripts of this gospel ascribe the hymn to

Elizabeth. Given the growth in Mariolatry in the early church and the development of the virgin birth tradition, the manuscripts that have Elizabeth's name are more likely to represent what Luke originally wrote. Scribes are less likely to have altered an original 'Mary' to 'Elizabeth'. In fact, a comparison of the Magnificat with Hannah's song in I Samuel 2 shows that the latter seems to have influenced the origin of the New Testament song. As Elizabeth is a type of Hannah (both are old barren women blessed in old age by an unexpected pregnancy through divine initiative), it is very probable that John the Baptist's followers adapted Hannah's song for their hero's mother to sing. Thus the Magnificat was originally applied not to Jesus, but to John the Baptist. The words immediately following the hymn in Luke 1.56 are more natural, and grammatically better, if Elizabeth is the author of the hymn.

III

Natural complements to the birth stories are the genealogies. Matthew begins his gospel with a genealogy; Luke inserts his after the account of Jesus' baptism, which suggests that Luke, like Mark, began the first draft of his gospel with the arrival of John the Baptist. It would seem that the main purpose of these genealogical lists was to connect Jesus with David; and to achieve this, the evangelists constructed lists based on Old Testament models. The Jewish roots of the historic Jesus and Jesus' parentage became increasingly important for the early church, paradoxically in the gospels written after AD 70, when the Jerusalem Temple and its associated cultus had been destroyed. Mark, written in the mid-to-late 60s, includes no genealogy; and Jesus' Jewishness and Messiahship are significantly underplayed at a time of rampant Jewish nationalism and opposition to Roman sovereignty. Mark's main reference to the Davidic descent of Jesus is in the saying in 12.35–37 where Jesus is made to deny that he is a 'Son of David'. Although this saying is found in the synoptic parallels, Matthew and Luke have no such apologia to make in their genealogies.

Luke's genealogy in 3.23–38 is an elaborate construction, designed to include eleven sets of seven names, even though, to achieve this symmetry, one name (Cainan) is duplicated. Luke, with his universalist interests, characteristically traces Jesus' origins to Adam, the father of mankind, unlike the pro-Jewish Matthew who takes Jesus' lineage back to Abraham, the father of the Jewish race. Luke begins his list with Jesus and works backward; Matthew starts with Abraham and goes forward to Jesus. But both evangelists trace Jesus' line through Joseph! This was, of course, natural. Jewish children were traced through the male line. Yet in Jesus' case this practice makes nonsense of the virgin birth story, and suggests that the genealogies were compiled before that tradition gained currency or, more probably, before that aspect of the birth had been invented.

When Luke prefaced his gospel with the birth stories, he was faced with the problem of his genealogy tracing Jesus through his father. Thus, Luke rather lamely added to his genealogy the words '(Jesus the son) *as was supposed* (of Joseph)'. Matthew's genealogy is as structured as Luke's, and confessedly so. He deliberately says there were fourteen generations between Abraham and David, fourteen from David to the deportation to Babylon, and fourteen from the deportation to Jesus. This arrangement is clearly not accurate. The last group spans some 600 years – and, in fact, contains only thirteen names! But fourteen is an important number in the context, as the Hebrew numerical values for the consonants of the name David total fourteen and gematria is characteristic of much Hebrew writing. Another indication of the unhistorical aspect of these lists is seen in comparing the two: Luke's genealogy has twenty-one names from Zerubbabel to Jesus – Matthew has twelve.

Mention of Mary in the genealogy at the beginning of Matthew's gospel may well imply at the least an irregularity in Jesus' birth. All the women mentioned in that genealogy had irregular marital unions yet despite this were instruments for God's messianic plans. The author of the genealogy was unable to end with the words 'Joseph begat Jesus'. Instead he writes '. . . Joseph the husband of Mary who gave birth to Jesus' and by showing there were precedents for Mary as a religious type the author deflects criticism. The virgin birth tradition also may have been another method of explaining the irregularity implied by Mary's pre-nuptial pregnancy. The Fourth Gospel (John 8.41) also implies that knowledge of Jesus' illegitimacy survived late.

The birth stories both in Matthew and Luke are unlikely to be historical. No item of substance in these chapters is verified elsewhere in the New Testament. Similarly it is unlikely that any of the material came from eye-witnesses or the original participators in the alleged events. Matthew's and Luke's accounts seem to have had a provenance independent from each other and both are theological and apologetic in intention not historical. The model for these narratives seems to be the Old Testament.

In Luke's account of the birth Mary's role is enhanced. Luke's purpose is to show that Jesus' miraculous birth was due to a virginal conception. In his genealogy Jesus is only the 'supposed' son of Joseph. It is in Luke's gospel that Mary is hailed by the angel as being full of grace. If Jesus is who Luke claims he is then his arrival must be of unique significance. Homage paid to Mary in the introduction is intended to enhance Jesus. Mary is honoured not for her own sake but for her unique role. Her place in Luke's narrative closely parallels Zechariah's in the birth of John the Baptist. John's birth is miraculous and Jesus who is depicted as greater than John must therefore be granted an even more miraculous birth. The words of the angel in Luke 1.28–31 and the words of Elizabeth (John's mother) to Mary in 1.42–45 reflect the early church's view of Jesus' birth. These words are later theological compositions, but it is these words which encouraged later elaboration of the person of Mary. But despite the comparatively honorific references to Mary, even in these chapters (1–2) it is possible that at 2.35 when Mary is told by Simeon directly that her heart will be pierced by a sword our author is drawing on the tradition of the break within the holy family. In Luke 12.49–53 Jesus says his mission in life is to sever family relationships. The parallel in Matthew 10.34–36 emphasizes this is because Jesus came to bring a sword. The poetic allusion in the infancy story may well reflect the anti-Mary trait in the tradition. A clearer example that Luke's infancy story is not so alienated from Mark's and Matthew's stories about the family is when Jesus in the temple at the age of twelve defines his true family (God) and his true home (the temple). His reluctance to return with his parents reflects an anti-Nazareth tradition comparable to the rejection story and is an anti-Mary development. In this story Mary understands neither Jesus' significance nor his words, despite the preceding revelation of his identity which we have just been told she has had twelve years on which to ponder! Mary's crass ignorance here is comparable to the disciples' lack of understanding throughout the gospels. Both features may be explained by the same bias. To this we shall turn in chapter 3.

Thus even in the infancy story in Luke's gospel Mary is not only a model for Christian obedience that many would wish to see in these chapters. There are here too the same traces of the attitude to be seen in Mark's and Matthew's gospels.

IV

Despite their lack of historicity, the stories of Jesus' birth proved to be masterpieces of pious writing. The inspiration that the story has given to countless believers, as well as to artists and dramatists, speaks for its effectiveness. Later church tradition embroidered the deceptively simple descriptions of Jesus' infancy in the gospels. Apocryphal tradition carried on the process initiated in the New Testament, and filled gaps in our knowledge of Jesus' career. Thus we have many stories about the child Jesus at work in his father's workshop. By and large these tales are bereft of theological significance and are either sentimental or full of magical or super-natural elements.

The New Testament itself leaves us with a tantalizing dark age between Jesus' infancy and his baptism. Luke alone among the canonical gospels sets one story in this period, – the story of Jesus in the Temple at the age of twelve (Luke 2.41–52). Although Luke may have hereby inspired the later apocryphal gospel writers to set other stories in Jesus' boyhood, Luke's intention in producing a story about Jesus at twelve was not to pad out knowledge about Jesus' forma-tive years. His purpose seems to have been, first, to show that Jesus was no mere Son of the Jewish Law (like other Jewish boys from the age of twelve), but that by calling the Temple 'his father's home' he was fulfilling his role as the Son *of God*. Here Luke is being character-istically universalist. Secondly, Luke's purpose was to draw attention, immediately before telling of Jesus' baptism and ministry, to the belief that Jesus' career would end with his resurrection. Far-fetched though this suggestion might seem, there are sufficient clues, both linguistic and symbolic, in Luke 2.41–52 to point us forward to the death and resurrection story. This apparently straightforward story cannot be taken on its face value as a childhood story; it is to some extent an allegory of the Easter faith, comparable in many ways with the walk to Emmaus.

Frustrating though it may be to lack essential background information about Jesus of Nazareth's birth and childhood, it would be improper to make use of the gospel's nativity stories as if these were historical or factual. If so much of the birth stories is secondary, late, legendary and unhistorical, and can be attributed to the literary, theological and biblical imagination of their authors, we may legitimately ask how much of Jesus' formative years and family background is ascertainable from the New Testament. The prospect of obtaining answers is bleak. Very little about Jesus' background or birth is known. The names of his parents and hometown are probably historic. Joseph never appears in the Bible outside the birth stories; but his name is fixed in the tradition despite the virgin birth stories intended to make his role redundant. John 1.45 knows of Jesus by his traditional name of 'Jesus son of Joseph from Nazareth'. In Luke 4.22 and John 6.42 Jesus is likewise referred to as 'son of Joseph'; the parallel in Matthew has 'son of the carpenter', and some manuscripts of Mark at 6.3 have as a secondary text an interesting alteration that makes Jesus himself the carpenter! Many scribes tended to avoid references to Joseph as Jesus' father. This scribal aberration in Mark is repeated on most occasions when the gospels speak naturally – despite the virgin birth traditions – of Joseph and Mary as Jesus' parents. Scribes alter 'parents' to 'Joseph and his mother'. Similarly, on occasions when the evangelists call Joseph 'his father', some manuscripts avoid this and write 'Joseph' instead. These textual variants are secondary, and were made to protect the virgin birth story throughout the gospel once this tradition became established in orthodox Christianity. The original text preserves the historic tradition that Jesus' father was named Joseph.

Jesus' brothers and sisters are referred to in Mark 3.31–35, and the brothers are named in Matthew 13.55. If we recognize that the virgin birth tradition is unhistorical and apologetic, then we need not imply, as some do, that brothers and sisters means half-brothers and half-sisters! One of the brothers, James, became leader of the Jerusalem church after Peter's strange disappearance. But despite, or because of, this rise to power, the majority of the references to Jesus' family in the gospels are derogatory. It is his family who try to arrest Jesus, and who claim he is mad (Mark 3.21). Jesus renounces his natural mother and siblings in his claim that whoever does the will of God is his family (Matt. 12.46–50). John 7.5 preserves a tradition that Jesus' brothers did not believe him. These traditions and attitudes seem very strange in the light of the birth narratives. They may, however, be explicable in so far as animosity against Jesus' family seems to reflect conditions when the pro-Pauline branch of the church sought to disparage the representatives of the Jerusalem church, which was headed by Jesus' brother, and in which Jesus' mother and the rest of his family were prominent (according to Acts 1.14). (To this we shall return in chapter 3.) The birth stories, on the other hand, were later compositions, written at a time when the need to separate Jesus from his historical milieu and his family was a less important factor. The old animosity fostered by Paul between the pro-gentile branch of the church and the pro-Jewish faction headed by Jesus' disciples and family was irrelevant when the nativity stories took shape. These narratives by contrast were concerned to emphasize Jesus' antecedents and origins. But, as we have seen, for all their apparent historicizing and verisimilitude, the Christmas story provides us with no more real facts about the historical Jesus than Paul himself does.

Texts
Luke 1–2; Matthew 1–2.

Bibliography
Raymond E. Brown, *The Birth of the Messiah*, Chapman 1977; J. Daniélou, *The Infancy Narratives*, Herder & Herder 1968; J. K. Elliott, 'Does Luke 2.41–52 Anticipate the Resurrection?', *Expository Times* 83, 1971–2, pp. 87–9; A. R. C. Leaney, 'The Birth Narratives in St Luke and St Matthew', *New Testament Studies* 8, 1961–2, pp. 158–66.

2 Who was John the Baptist?

If John the Baptist had attracted better propagandists, the religious movement he founded could have rivalled Christianity – and even overtaken it in popularity. Just how popular John was is not always obvious from the New Testament. That is because the writers of the Christian scriptures altered the historical details about John to suit their own ends. With the exception of a few references to John in one or two non-Christian documents, we are really dependent on the New Testament for historical evidence about John the Baptist and his movement. But because of the theological bias of the New Testament we cannot accept its evidence uncritically.

When looking behind the finished gospels, one has to peel away the layers of tradition underlying them – especially if one is trying to expose their historical kernel. In the case of the traditions surrounding John the Baptist, the reader needs to appreciate that there are at least four layers. First there is the historic John; secondly, the traditions about John as put out by John's disciples; thirdly, these traditions as reinterpreted by Jesus' followers; and fourthly, the use made of these traditions by the individual gospel writers in the New Testament. We must be alert to the probability that each rewriting distorted the traditions, in some cases changing the historical facts.

Apart from the account of his birth (in Luke) and his death (in Mark and Matthew), it is difficult to harmonize or reconcile the rest of John's story because of the differing accounts in the gospels. There are too many discrepancies. For instance, did John in fact baptize Jesus? Matthew and Mark say Yes; Luke says No; and the Fourth Gospel is non-committal. Another question is 'Did John and

Jesus work together?' The Fourth Gospel describes a parallel ministry, with John and Jesus both baptizing; the other evangelists say that John was imprisoned before Jesus began his ministry, and give no indication that Jesus was ever a baptist. Another area of disagreement between the gospels is the role John is said to fulfil – was he the new Elijah, or not?

Whenever we read the Bible for historical research, we come across difficulties of this sort. That is because the New Testament was written from a theological standpoint; historical events were made use of, but are subsidiary to the religious interests of the writers. Each of the gospel writers had his own theological inclination. He certainly made use of oral and written material in order to write his books; but this was often adapted in the process for a variety of reasons.

In reconstructing the contemporary situation, it must be remembered that early Christians were determined to promote Jesus as the true Messiah, and to win converts to this belief. Christians were those who believed that Jesus of Nazareth was the one and only Messiah. But there had been several claimants for this title, especially in the first century. The Roman domination of Palestine at that time encouraged many nationalists, as well as apocalyptic pipe-dreamers, to look back to the golden days of Israel. Some wanted a new David to restore Israel to its former glory. Others looked for a supernatural figure who would deliver Israel from its oppressors and lead it to a glorious kingdom of God. Christians saw Jesus as such a deliverer, and they denounced all other claimants as anti-Christs. These false prophets are vigorously condemned in the New Testament and one such false Christ seems to have been John the Baptist.

Luke's gospel records (3.15) that when John the Baptist came on the scene he was identified by some as the Messiah. Whether John himself ever claimed to be Messiah is unknown, but some people certainly saw him as such. These were the people who are identified as 'the disciples of John' on several occasions in the gospels. The Christians had to convince such people they were wrong – and that only Jesus fitted that particular role. This is partly why the New Testament gospels were composed.

It seems as if the Christians encountered strongest opposition to their claim that Jesus was Messiah from this rival group who were attached to the memory of John the Baptist, and who were as determined as the Christians to promote their own candidate.

So the Christians set out to woo John's disciples away from supporting John by showing them who John the Baptist really was and by stressing that he was inferior to Jesus who (according to them) was the only true Lord and Messiah. This rivalry was taking place long after John and Jesus themselves had died. We may assume that the traditional date of both men's deaths (in the early thirties of the first century) is correct. The competitiveness occurred later between their supporters.

To convince John's followers, the Christians made use of the traditions and stories about John that were in circulation, and adapted them to suit their own needs. Similarly, stories were created in which contact between John and Jesus, or between their followers, enabled the Christians to state their view of the identity of both men. The Christians were also keen to state that the church was the only true heir of John's teaching, and that those who followed only John had missed the point of his teaching. The stories about John (and his disciples) in the Christian gospels were therefore written from the point of view of later Christian apologetics and with the aim of converting John's followers.

The Christian writers of the gospels tried to impose a strict demarcation line between who John was and who Jesus was. This met with varying degrees of success, depending on how thoroughly the writer reworked the tradition. Basically what it came down to was that if Jesus was the Christ, then John the Baptist must be Elijah.

The reason why John was allotted this title was because, at that time, it had become part of Jewish teaching that, before the end of the world, Elijah, the great Old Testament prophet, would reappear to prepare the way for God. In Christian eyes Jesus had already initiated and ushered in the endtime, and thus the Elijah must have already come. And who better to fulfil that role than John? Thus it fitted the Christians' point of view to think of John as Elijah – the forerunner of Christ.

There was perhaps some historical justification for seeing John in this way. If the gospels' picture of John in the wilderness is in any sense an accurate one, then John may well have set out to be the new Elijah. The mode of dress, the ascetic habits, and, more particularly, his work in the wilderness would have encouraged Jews to identify John as a prophet in the Old Testament mould, and as an Elijah in particular.

Again, if the gospels are right in telling us that John's basic purpose in life was to purify the Jews and prepare them for the last judgment, then they would be presenting a view entirely appropriate and compatible with that of Elijah in the apocalyptic literature. Certainly John's basic purpose seems to have been to encourage Jews to confess their sins and to be purified by an act of baptism administered by his hands. John may well have been chosen to perform the role of a returned Elijah. At any rate, that is how at least some of the New Testament writers were prepared to describe him, if for no other reason than that it was a convenient way of giving John some degree of importance.

This demarcation was therefore imposed on the oral, and perhaps written, traditions that reached the Christian writers, but not always entirely successfully. In several places in the New Testament contradictory statements about the identity of the two men, John and Jesus, shine through. Mark 6.14–16; 8.27–29; Luke 1.68–69 and John 1.19–27 are passages where we learn not only that *Jesus* was sometimes thought of as Elijah, a reincarnated John the Baptist, or a prophet, but also that the Baptist was spoken of in Messianic terms as if he were the Christ. In other words, until the gospel writers tried, albeit imperfectly, to impose some order on the material, there were traditions in existence attributing to both John and Jesus similar titles.

As far as the identification of Jesus with Elijah is concerned, Luke's gospel in particular betrays evidence that at least at one stage in the tradition such an identification was intended. If one reads the difficult story in Luke 9.51–56 where a Samaritan village refuses to entertain Jesus, two of his disciples ask Jesus if they can call down fire from heaven to burn the village. This story seems to have been based on a passage in the Old Testament (II Kings 1.9–12) when Elijah commands a consuming fire to come from heaven. Two other stories in this gospel enable us to connect Jesus with Elijah. In the episode of Jesus in Nazareth in Luke 4.16–30 he is made to compare his actions with those of Elijah in dealing with widows in Israel. This may have also motivated Luke in telling the story of the healing of the widow's son (7.11–17) in so far as Elijah is said to have healed a widow's son in II Kings 1.9. This passage in II Kings might also have been responsible for Jesus like Elijah stating 'I have come to set fire on earth'. This is perhaps not our normal picture of Jesus, but if Jesus was thought at one time to be the new Elijah he had to be made to act like Elijah, whose role was to bring fire and judgment.

Once Jesus was presented as bringing not these qualities but deliverance and love (themes more acceptable for the early church to export and win converts with) then the role of Elijah would not be considered a suitable or helpful analogy. That is probably why the role of Elijah was transferred in at least some portions of the New Testament to John the Baptist.

Such a transfer would no doubt have been responsible for encouraging the popularity of the Transfiguration account (Mark 9.2–8). In the story Jesus climbs a mountain and meets Moses and Elijah. What is being symbolized is that Jesus supersedes the law (personified by Moses) and the prophets (represented by Elijah). There is no identification of Jesus with Elijah: Jesus is greater. This should have stopped further stories associating Jesus with Elijah and left the way clear for John the Baptist to be so identified. What is surprising is that this point has not permeated all the gospel material. As we have seen, the tradition which that story was intended to quash (that is that Jesus was Elijah) is still apparent.

For the Christians, the picture of Jesus as Elijah was inadequate. They needed to portray him as something greater. Hence the figure of the Messiah was the obvious one to come to the minds of these Christians of Jewish background.

One line of thinking promulgated possibly by John the Baptist's followers questioned Jesus' eligibility for the Messiahship. John 7.41 shows that some doubted Jesus' pedigree. The argument there is: if Jesus is the Messiah, then he ought to be of the lineage of David and have been born in accordance with Messianic expectation in Bethlehem. Jesus was of course known to be from Nazareth in the northern province of the Galilee – a detail which seems historic and is firmly fixed in the tradition.

This obstacle to belief in Jesus as Messiah had to be countered. So the Christian apologists got to work. The doubts expressed in John 7.41 had been current for a long time. Much earlier than the

Fourth Gospel the birth stories attached to Matthew's and Luke's gospels were composed precisely to combat the doubts of John 7.41 as we saw in chapter 1. The nativity stories set out to show among other things that Jesus was born in Bethlehem. Using legendary and traditional material to fill in this essential piece of background both evangelists succeed in producing totally differing accounts of how Jesus was born in the right place – the Davidic city of Bethlehem.

It is difficult to assess historically how conscious either man was in fulfilling any particular role or function. We have only the gospels to work from, and these are, as we have seen, overlaid with differing layers of tradition and interpretation. Let us work back, however, to what *could* have been the likeliest historical sequence.

The New Testament statement that John's ministry predated Jesus' is probably correct. So, too, is the belief that Jesus was baptized by John. Baptism as a rite was known in sectarian Judaism at the time, and was used, for example, by the Dead Sea Scroll community as a regular and ceremonial lustration. It was also administered to non-Jewish proselytes as an initiation into Judaism. Where John was distinctive, and why he became known by the rite, is that he baptized *Jews* in a once-and-for-all act. The Christians are unlikely to have invented the story of Jesus being baptized; and the way it is told in the two earliest gospels – Mark and Matthew – is in opposition to the normal anti-Baptist polemic that is dominant elsewhere.

In Mark's account of the baptism (1.6–11) Jesus seems to be inferior to John in so far as he *submits* himself to John's baptism. And, according to Mark, it is as a result of his baptism at John's hands that Jesus received his commission to preach on his own. In other words, Jesus is powerless until he meets John. The theological difficulties in Mark's baptism story have taxed theologians since it was written. The main problem has been why a man described as Son of God, and thereby assumed to be without sin, submitted himself to a rite intended by John as a baptism for the remission of sins. Various explanations, which do not concern us here, have been offered. For us, the fact that such difficulties are created by Mark's account tells in favour of its underlying historicity.

The difficulties and embarrassment created by Mark's account are seen in Matthew's re-telling of Mark's story. He has John demur at the thought of baptizing Jesus, of all people, by saying 'I have need rather to be baptized by you'; and Jesus has to reassure him.

In the later gospels, Luke and the Fourth Gospel, the story has been further refined. Luke avoids saying Jesus submitted himself to John's baptism by using a passive verb: 'During a general baptism of the people, when Jesus too *had been baptized* . . .' Thus he does not need to say by whom! And just in case readers might assume John was responsible, Luke precedes this story by telling us that John the Baptist was already in prison by this time. The Fourth Gospel goes even further, and removes the account of the baptism of Jesus. It is implied merely with a statement on John's lips that, while he, John, was baptizing he saw the spirit of God descend on Jesus. There is no connection here with the actual baptism of Jesus.

The one certain thing we can say about Jesus and John in Mark's baptism story is that Jesus' motive in joining John is that he approved of John's aims and identified himself with his movement. Jesus' solidarity with John's movement is also seen in John 10.40 where Jesus continues preaching in John's area.

We could go further, however, and suggest that John and Jesus worked together for a period, and that Jesus was one of John's disciples. When John is represented as stating, as he does on several occasions, that 'the one who follows after me is mightier', he might not be speaking chronologically. He may be calling Jesus his disciple – 'the one who follows', was a common way of referring to a disciple.

Apart from the legendary stories of Jesus' birth (and the equally spurious story of Jesus in the temple at the age of twelve) the gospels tell us nothing about the period before Jesus' own public ministry. Matthew, Mark and Luke date Jesus' ministry from his initiation through baptism; but there may well have been a longer interval than the forty days in the wilderness suggested by the temptations narrative in the New Testament (Mark 1.12–13). John and Jesus may have worked together for a long time before Jesus branched out on his own. This view is consistent with the Fourth Gospel, but contradicts the other gospels, where John is imprisoned before Jesus begins his ministry.

Assuming the Fourth Gospel is correct in saying John and Jesus worked alongside each other for a while, we must speculate why the two men split. A possible explanation is that Jesus became aware that he was the Coming One about whom John was preaching. He then succeeded in convincing many of his contemporaries that the one whom John said they were to prepare for was, in fact, himself. Perhaps at first Jesus also set out to play the role of the prophet Elijah; and this would explain the emergence of those traditions that identify Jesus in this way. But certainly by the time Jesus paid his last visit to Jerusalem, his role had changed. With the triumphal entry, Jesus is Messiah. It is as king of the Jews he enters Jerusalem, and it is as such he is killed. If the triumphal entry was an historic event, then here is an episode in which Jesus set out deliberately to enact an Old Testament prophecy in which the Messiah as King enters meekly seated on a colt (Matt. 21.1–9).

Many of the disciples of John were unwilling to see Jesus as Messiah. Not only was the carpenter's son from Nazareth unlikely to be the long-awaited Messiah; but his actions seemed not to fit in with what John had said the Coming One would do. This latter point is evident in the story in Matthew 11, in which John in prison asks Jesus through his disciples if he is the Coming One. The answer given here is that Jesus does indeed fulfil Messianic expectations by healing the sick. This conversation, read back into the life of John and Jesus by the evangelists, reflects one pattern of dialogue used by the Christians in their discussions with John's followers.

Another way of answering the doubts about Jesus raised by John's followers was to repeat stories in which John himself recognizes Jesus as the Coming One and identifies him as such. This is no doubt the origin of John 1.29–30, where the Baptist says Jesus is the Coming One. The Fourth Gospel tries to nail the problem by having John give evidence on behalf of the Christians against the doubters among his followers. The question from prison and the reply in Matthew's gospel is more primitive, in so far as dialogue with the disciples of John is still open-ended. By the time the Fourth Gospel was written, twenty years had lapsed and attitudes had hardened: John's disciples and Jesus' had taken up entrenched positions.

The main reason why John's followers were unwilling to accept Jesus as the Coming One was not that Jesus had overdone things by claiming that he was the Coming One, and that the Coming One was the Messiah, but that as such his behaviour contrasted too much with John's asceticism. We are told in the gospels that John's movement was characterized by prayer and fasting. That Jesus' followers were not required to be of this type was one of the causes of the split between the two groups. Jesus' followers felt that fasting was inappropriate. Once they were convinced they had Jesus the Messianic bridegroom among them they behaved like wedding guests. The fasting of John's group was not remarkable in itself. It is mentioned in the New Testament only because it was a significant mark of difference between Jesus and his erstwhile master John. The exuberance of the early Christians caused by their distinctive belief contrasted with the cheerlessness of John's movement and its message.

But both movements developed from the same root, and there are consequently many similarities between both groups and both leaders, which is doubtless why confusion occurred. Both were contemporaries, both were Jews, working outside the mainstream of Judaism and both were concerned to establish the rule of God on earth. This similarity may be illustrated by the story (Mark 11.27–33) in which Jesus' authority was questioned by the Jewish religious leaders. Jesus' reply compares his own authority to the authority John the Baptist possessed. The story implies that it was popularly agreed that John was divinely inspired. Here John (and his followers) and Jesus (and his) are placed on the same side against the establishment. The story was doubtless promoted by Christians determined to place Jesus on the same level of popular belief as John.

Likewise, both men are together in opposition to the cynicism of the world at large. Matthew 11.16–19 places John and Jesus on the same side of the religious fence. In trying to win converts, the Christians obviously approached John's disciples initially in so far as they were closer in aim than the masses outside. In the eyes of the earliest Christians John's disciples were half way there – they just needed extra persuasion that Jesus was the Coming One of John's preaching.

Among other similarities, both men attracted disciples to themselves, and both men met violent deaths. The influence and memory of both men lingered on after their deaths so much so that the resurrection of both men was considered as possible.

The transference of disciples from one group to another also suggests a closeness. We are told in the Fourth Gospel (John 1.40) that Andrew and Simon Peter had been disciples of John the Baptist before they joined Jesus' group. Similarly, the choice of Judas' successor as the twelfth man in the team of close disciples seems to have been restricted to those who had first been disciples of John (Acts 1.22).

Wooing the followers of John appears to have been the aim of much Christian writing. Two episodes in the Acts of the Apostles show that the church was determined to win over erstwhile members of John's movement. Acts 18.24–28 introduces us to Apollos, who, like Simon and Andrew earlier, had been a follower of the Baptist, but then had been 'instructed in the way of the (real) Lord'.

This passage is then followed by an episode alleged to have occurred in Ephesus, where Paul meets a group of John's followers. The Baptist movement had therefore spread, like Christianity, into Asia Minor. Paul tells them that they must accept that the Coming One, of whom their leader spoke, had arrived in the person of Jesus of Nazareth. On hearing this, they, not surprisingly in this book, became baptized as Christians. Acts obviously found this a useful tale to spur on the missionary zeal of its readers.

The rivalry between the two groups, John's and Jesus', is evident in other places in the New Testament as well. Anything John is reputed (by his followers) to have said or done, Jesus is said (by his followers) to have surpassed.

There is, in fact, little of John's teaching in the New Testament, except for those passages where John points to Jesus' superiority; but there is some, which in itself is rather surprising. This teaching may well have originated in pre-Christian or non-Christian circles, which does not mean that the teaching attributed to John is any more historical than that attributed to Jesus; but what we can say is that it is likely to have come originally from John's circle.

Much of the teaching in John's major speech in Matthew 3 is repeated elsewhere in that gospel with *Jesus* as the speaker. The motive for repeating John's words on Jesus' lips seems to be that the Christians wished to win over John's disciples by, among other things, using some of *their* leader's teaching, and pointing out that Jesus stood for the same principles as John.

In John's speech in Matthew 3 three things are put on John's lips. (a) His opening words are 'Repent for the kingdom of God is upon you' but they are not exclusive to John. Jesus' opening words at the start of *his* ministry (Matt. 4.17) are identical. (b) John and Jesus both are attributed with strong words of denunciation against the Pharisees and Sadducees. John here in chapter 3 and Jesus later both call them 'You brood of vipers'. (c) Thirdly John in this speech says that every tree which fails to produce good fruit is to be cut down and burnt. Jesus is to say the same later. All three sayings belong more comfortably to John's mission than to Jesus'.

Another place where the Christians seem to have appropriated material from John's group is the famous prayer 'Our Father which art in heaven . . .'. This is usually referred to as 'The Lord's Prayer' as if it originated with Jesus. But, historically, it seems to have emanated from John. The explanation lies in the introduction to the prayer in Luke 11.1. There, the disciples ask Jesus to teach them to pray *as John taught his disciples*. Now, as Jews, Jesus' disciples would know *how* to pray – and, in fact, in several places in the gospels Jesus assumes that they will pray. What is meant in Luke 11.1 is that the disciples of Jesus ask for the special prayer that John is known to have used. From this Baptist background, therefore, came the so-called Lord's prayer. In the gospels Jesus gets the credit for introducing it. But he is likely to have learnt it from John during the time he was one of John's disciples.

Just as teaching originating with John's movement is placed on Jesus' lips in order to present him as the originator, so speeches are attributed to John by the Christians that have the purpose of enhancing Jesus. In particular John's swansong in the Fourth Gospel is 'I will decrease but he (Jesus) will increase'. This is what the Christians wanted to see happen; and they used John as a spokesman for their own ideas. The church wanted John as a witness to Christ against his own disciples. The Christians, therefore, tried to make John himself condemn the *raison d'être* for his own movement.

The ease with which stories originating in John's circle were taken over by Jesus' followers for their own ends is particularly conspicuous in the birth narratives in Luke 1–2. We are all familiar with the Christmas story; but it is interesting to compare the story of John the Baptist's birth with the story of Jesus' birth. Such a study reveals many parallels between what is said about John and about Jesus, usually to Jesus' advantage. This common material is not due to mere coincidence, or to the similarity between the two men historically, but to Christians adapting stories about John.

Let us repeat from chapter 1 some of these parallels. Both John's and Jesus' birth is announced by an angel, who begins by telling both Zechariah (John's father) and Mary (Jesus' mother) not to be afraid. He tells both parents independently that their offspring will be great. Both births are said to be spiritually encouraged. The two sets of stories have also been linked by Luke rather artificially by stating that Mary and Elizabeth (John's mother) were related. There are other parallels too.

But, despite the comparability of the two stories, the aim of the Christian adapter of the stories about John is to stress John's inferiority. Even though the announcement of Jesus' birth is dated from the conception of John, when the two pregnant women are said to meet, Elizabeth's baby 'leaps for joy' in her womb in praise of Mary's baby.

It would seem as if John's followers had adapted some earlier Messianic hymns and prophecies and applied them to John. It is in these chapters of Luke that the highest praise of John is found in the Bible. For instance see the Benedictus in Luke 1.68–69. Only once in these chapters is John spoken of as Elijah, which may well be a Christian interpolation; mostly he is addressed in Messianic terms.

The Christians in building up birth stories for their leader did the same sort of thing, that is, they took Messianic hymns and applied them to Jesus.

John's movement had preceded Jesus'; hence the stories about his birth were in existence as soon as John had become a cult figure. Only the most important men had birth stories prefacing the legends about them. Luke is likely to have made use of stories about John in order to write a parallel account concerning the birth of Jesus.

Another instance where Christians had to enhance Jesus over John is as a baptist! The earliest Christians, as today, were initiated into the faith by the rite of baptism. The reason for this was because many of the first Christians, like Jesus himself, had previously been disciples of John and as such had been baptized into his movement. When Jesus set up his own group, it is likely that baptizing converts into this new movement remained the mark of initiation, except that converts were baptized into *Jesus'* name.

But when the gospels were being written, and the rivalry between the two groups was at its highest, the Christians seemed to have been embarrassed that the origin of this baptism was with John. Two solutions to this difficulty were written into the gospels. One was to say that Christians were baptized not because they were following John's example, but because Jesus commanded it. This solution is found at the very end of Matthew's gospel.

The other way was to say that the Christians baptized because they were following Jesus' own example. The Fourth Gospel favours this solution. In John 3.22–4.1 when John and Jesus had separated and were pursuing their own ministries, both are said to be baptizing converts. We are naturally told that 'Jesus is winning and baptizing more disciples than John'!

Another area where the Christians had to deny that John had any influence was as a miracle worker. There are in fact no accounts of John in this role extant in the gospels, and John 10.41 has the crowds say that John unlike Jesus 'gave us no miraculous sign'. This denial, on the analogy with other contradictions, presumably means that some were prepared to see John the Baptist as a signgiver and as a wonder-worker. Again we see how this gospel in particular was concerned to deny to the Baptist any title or attribute which ought properly to belong to Jesus only.

Having been confronted by this developing and, in many ways, distorted picture of John and Jesus in the gospels, we can now see how that tradition was built up. The first layer – the historical context – has John the Baptist behaving very much like an Old Testament prophet, calling Jews to repentance as a preparation for the end of the world and the coming of the Lord. The second level in the tradition came from John's circle – probably after his death. His followers, unable to accept the claims made by and for Jesus, tended to idolize John and to think of him either as Elijah or the Messiah. Stories and traditions emphasizing John's importance developed with this aim in view. The stories of John's birth and death came from this movement.

The third stage in the formation of the New Testament narratives came with the Christian reinterpretation of the legends and sayings attached to John. The general tendency was to play down the exalted references to John, and to emphasize that it was Jesus and Jesus alone who was the Lord and Messiah.

The fourth stage came when the individual evangelists got to work on the tradition, and found their own particular way of fitting John into the Christian pattern. John was obviously too important a figure in the early church to be ignored, and his followers needed converting. Thus some gospel writers emphasized that John was the new Elijah preceding the Messiah. This solution was not entirely satisfactory and was not whole-heartedly accepted throughout the tradition. Some parts of the New Testament kept John the Baptist and the Elijah as separate figures; and the Fourth Gospel has John deny he is the Elijah. But as Matthew says 'if you are willing to accept it' (and many were not) John could be thought of as the Elijah.

But however exalted a role the Elijah figure was, and however influential and important John was as a prophet, the gospels took care to point out that he was only a representative of the *Old* Testament. John was pre-Christian, and as such was inferior to Christ and to Christ's followers. A compliment in Matthew's gospel begins by stating – no doubt to the approval of John's followers – 'Among those born of woman there is no one greater than John the Baptist', but Matthew caps this slogan by stating that the least in the kingdom of Heaven (that is, those who follow Christ) is greater than John.

Luke's gospel divides time into two: the period up to John, and the period since Christ. John is the last and greatest of the prophets and to that extent the Old Testament ends with him. The New Testament starts with Christ (Luke 16.16).

Even the Fourth Gospel had to find something positive to say about John the Baptist that would satisfy the aspirations of his followers and take account of his evident influence and importance. This is why John is made the first witness to Christ. He is consistently portrayed as the one who points to and identifies Jesus as such. The Fourth Gospel mentions neither John's birth nor death: he is significant only for his witness. The passages in the Acts of the Apostles dealing with John show that the early Christian preachers, too, thought of John in this way.

This portrayal satisfied Christians thereafter. It was because John was a witness to Christ that the church adopted him – and eventually canonized him. Churches throughout the world have been dedicated to St John the Baptist mainly because they see themselves – as the early Christians saw John – as a pointer to Christ.

The later history of John the Baptist's sect goes beyond the New Testament period and is referred to, among other places, in the so-called pseudo-Clementine Recognitions dating from about 230, in the Slavonic additions to Josephus' *The Jewish War* and in Mandaean literature. The Christians themselves were responsible for other legends preserved in the writings of the church fathers and in the apocryphal literature. But, ironically, the most significant and in many ways the most historical sourcebook for our knowledge about John the Baptist is in the New Testament, the very collection that was written, among other things, to place John's name and influence in a lower rank.

Texts

Matthew 3; 11.2–19; Mark 1.1–11; 6.14–29; 8.27–29; Luke 1; John 1.6–42; 4.1–2.

Bibliography

C. Scobie, *John the Baptist*, SCM Press 1964; W. Wink, *John the Baptist in the Gospel Tradition*, Society for New Testament Study Monograph VII, Cambridge University Press 1968.

3 The Ministry and Teaching of Jesus

Having been a disciple of John the Baptist Jesus broke away and founded a rival movement with himself as its head. In so doing Jesus assumed the role of the Messiah and set himself up as the 'one who is to come' promised by John. Jesus then left the wilderness with some of John's former adherents and went into the Galilee to preach the imminence of the kingdom of God, gathering to him other followers. The gospels devote most of their contents to Jesus' preaching and ministry.

The duration of Jesus' ministry is not certain. Tradition conventionally assumes it lasted three years, because the Fourth Gospel refers to three visits by Jesus to Jerusalem for the Passover (2.13; 6.4; 12.1). The synoptic gospels do not tell of visits to Jerusalem during the ministry and we must suspect John's chronology. His theological motives require Jesus to be more intimately connected with Jerusalem than is the case with the earlier gospels. This means we cannot fix our chronology of Jesus' ministry on these references to the Passover in John's gospel.

I

Most of the gospel material appears in separate isolated paragraphs which contain within themselves neither time references nor, in many cases, geographical details. Many of the individual paragraphs especially in the synoptic gospels have no connexion with the paragraphs preceding or following, and may indeed appear in a different sequence. The gospels of Matthew, Mark and Luke contain many stories in common and it is interesting to compare them noting the differences in content and context, and the differing sequence in which the same stories sometimes occur. This should not be surprising if it is recognized that most of the stories and sayings in those gospels originally circulated orally among the early Christian communities. It is only when these stories were collected together and written down that editorial decisions needed to be taken about the sequence and relative order in which the paragraphs were to appear.

The gospel writers, lacking in the majority of stories any precise details about the place in Jesus' career when the story should occur, were primarily motivated by dramatic or theological considerations. Each writer had his own conception of the best sequence.

Sometimes the authors were guided by themes, and it is interesting to note how many stories are linked by a common reference or catchphrase. Several stories for instance are set on or around the Lake of Gennesaret as can be seen in Mark 4.1, 35; 5.1, 21. Similarly many isolated sayings, the original contexts of which were lost, were conveniently linked to form the so-called great sermon of Matt. 5–7 or Luke 6.17–49. Even if all the sayings contained in these sermons were spoken by Jesus it is improbable that he delivered himself of them in one sitting. Matthew having collected several dominical sayings wrote them as one sermon on the model of Moses on Sinai. For instance he has Jesus climb a mountain to deliver his sermon: this then begins with the Beatitudes which parallel the decalogue. The artificiality of Matthew's plan is apparent in that he has Jesus begin the sermon speaking to the disciples and end it talking to the crowds. Luke who has less interest in portraying Jesus as the second Moses avoids Matthew's plan and has Jesus deliver a shorter sermon, in which many of the sayings differ from those in Matthew's collection and this is located on a level place.

The problem faced by the evangelists was not only that they inherited sayings and stories most of which had no internal details about their original context but they themselves were unlikely to have known Jesus. Church tradition tried to give the gospels apostolic authority by attributing their authorship to followers of Jesus or Paul. Thus the third gospel was attributed to Luke the companion of Paul. The author of the second gospel is said to have been Peter's interpreter. The gospels do not contain within themselves any clue about the name or identity of their author except John 21.24 which suggests that the author of at least that chapter is the beloved disciple, but he is not identified more precisely. The titles to the gospels were scribal additions and did not form part of the autographs.

If the gospel writers had known Jesus or followed him during his ministry it is unlikely they would have differed so much in detail in the stories they have in common. Similarly had they been witnesses to the events they relate it is improbable that they would have relied on previous written sources. The so-called synoptic problem is caused by a comparative analysis of the gospels of Matthew, Mark and Luke where on the one hand many of the verses are identical even to the extent of their having the same Greek particle in common but on the other hand many stories in one gospel are unique or have only a tenuous link with a similar story in another gospel. The problem is to find a reason for both the similarities and differences. The usual solution is to posit direct literary interdependence. Many solutions have been proposed, the most common being that Mark's gospel because of its style and theology was written first and was then used and copied independently by both Matthew and Luke in the composition of their own gospels. The later evangelists also made use of other material at their disposal most of which might like Mark have already been in writing. To explain similarities between Matthew and Luke alone it is not certain if Luke used Matthew or whether these two gospels had in common another written source. If such a hypothetical document ever existed alongside Mark it is no longer extant as an independent work. Nevertheless many scholars are prepared to explain that the similarities between Matthew's and Luke's gospels are due to their using this hypothetical source, normally labelled 'Q', just as they made use of Mark, rather than to argue that Luke read and used Matthew's gospel.

Even the Fourth Gospel which betrays such marked differences from the synoptics is not entirely independent of them and has some material in common which could have entered this work indirectly through John's familiarity with the synoptics' material. Although scholars disagree about the relative order in which the gospels were written both in this chapter and the rest of this book the sequence Mark, Matthew, Luke and John is adopted.

The dates when these gospels were written is also in dispute but the consensus of scholarly opinion puts Mark at 65, Matthew and Luke 75–85 and John towards the end of the century. These dates are assumed in this book. This means that the earliest gospel, Mark, although possibly drawing on material already in existence in written form, such as the apocalyptic discourse of chapter 13, or even the passion narrative, was not composed until thirty years after the traditional date of the crucifixion. It also means that Mark's gospel is later than Paul's epistles. The latest gospel, John, was composed sixty years after the crucifixion. Thus it is not surprising that differences between the accounts of Jesus' ministry emerged.

The gospels therefore were compiled much later than the events they tell of and the material in them is in many cases derivative. The accuracy and historicity of the gospel material is not to be assumed. Despite the alleged retentiveness of the oriental memory – a phenomenon made use of *ad nauseam* by fundamentalists determined at all costs to avoid challenges to the factualness of the New Testament – in works of theology such as the gospels accuracy of fact and precision of reporting are not prime considerations. Religious truths need not always be expressed in terms of objective factuality. This means that we cannot read through the gospels accepting uncritically their accounts of Jesus' ministry.

It is improbable that Jesus' followers deliberately noted down exactly what Jesus did or learned precisely what he taught. In addition the thirty year gap between these events and the first written account of them makes us doubt the historical worth of much in the gospels. In that gap some stories were developed as they spread among the Hellenistic church, and others were invented. The writing of the gospels merely represents a final stage in the progression of stories about Jesus. Each gospel was written within a Christian community and is a theological document making use of some of the written and oral material that came its way in order to produce a homogeneous entity at a time when the need to have a permanent record of what Jesus did and said was created by the missionary activities of the developing church. The gospels as well as making their own theological statements acted as a guide to orthodoxy in their own community, as a fixing of the tradition on the basis of the communities' memory, practices or experiences, and also as a handbook for its members and missionaries.

During the period of oral transmission elaborations and distortions of the original material occurred. Stories compatible with what was known of the earthly Jesus were added to the tradition. Other stories and sayings were adjusted to fit changing circumstances. The written gospels enable us to compare differences within the same stories and reveal how changes occurred, for example groups of people often unnamed or unidentified in one gospel gather names as the tradition develops. The unnamed people who object to the waste of money at the anointing of Jesus in Mark 14.4 are identified as 'the disciples' in Matt. 26.8. Even greater precision is achieved in the retelling of the story in the Fourth Gospel which not surprisingly focusses attention on one disciple – Judas (John 12.4). Similarly in that story the woman who anoints Jesus is not named by Mark despite his statement (14.9) that her action will make her world famous! John supplies her name, Mary. In other stories those who accuse Jesus are given names. As the gospel tradition developed we read of different groups of accusers, sometimes Pharisees, sometimes scribes, at other times priests. One suspects that in the earliest traditions these groups were not named and that Jesus merely met opposition possibly from Jews.

On some occasions elaboration of detail is a sure sign of the developing tradition. The man with the withered hand in Mark 3.1 has his *right* hand withered in Luke 6.6. The dead son of Mark 6.17 becomes an only child in Luke 9.38. The one demoniac of Mark 5.1–20 becomes two in Matt. 8.28–34 although both act and speak in unison. Similarly the one blind man of Mark's story (10.46–52) becomes two in Matthew's parallel (Matt. 20.39–34). One may assume that if such changes and elaboration occur within the written tradition similar phenomena may be found in the pre-literary stage of the gospel transmission. Elaboration is however not the only phenomenon to be detected. Occasionally pruning occurs: Mark's verbose telling of the feeding of the 5000 or of the Gadarene maniac is drastically doctored in the later accounts.

The material in the Fourth Gospel is often very different from that in the synoptics. John's style and presentation especially of Jesus' sayings are obviously more meditative and philosophical than the synoptics' but this does not brand these earlier accounts as necessarily more reliable. *All four* are adaptations of existing traditions.

Each Christian community either remembered or invented stories and sayings about Jesus that suited its own purposes. One of the main preoccupations of the increasingly gentile missionary activity in the early church was the extent to which Jewish observances were relevant for non-Jewish Christians. Thus it is not surprising to find stories in the gospels in which Jesus makes pronouncements about such matters as the sabbath (Mark 2.23–28; 3.1–5; Luke 13.10–17; John 5.9), taxpaying (Mark 12.13–17; Matt. 17.24–27), fasting (Mark 2.18–22), table-fellowship (Mark 2.15–17; Luke 11.37–41), food regulations (Mark 7.1–8). These and similar debates reflect the controversies within the nascent church. They are problems which Paul wrestles with in his epistles. The birth pangs of Christianity involved first a loosening and then a severing of ties with Judaism. These are reflected in the gospels where the controversies are written up as scenes involving the earthly Jesus in debates with Pharisees just as the gentile churches that produced these dramatizations were in debate with Jews and Jewish Christians. The contrived and artificial nature of these encounters between Jesus and Jewish groups is evident in the gospels in scenes such as the debate in the cornfield (Mark 2.24) when Pharisees on the sabbath are depicted lurking in the middle of the fields for the express purpose of accusing Jesus!

The relevance of such stories for the early Christians was obvious. For them it was important to have in their written records a statement about Jesus' attitude to such controversies in order to quell opposition to their practice. Many of the sayings of Jesus recorded in the gospels reflect the preoccupations of the early church and can be seen as those communities' rules and laws re-enforced by a dominical pronouncement.

Other material in the gospels reflects the missionary activity and experiences of the earliest disciples. This matter also belongs to the post-Easter church and although it is written into the life of the earthly Jesus, whose opinions and pronouncements they believed they were faithfully following, it is also unlikely to be historical or reproduce the *ipsissima verba* of Jesus. The instructions given to the twelve disciples in Luke 9 and to the seventy or seventy-two in chapter 10 (the text of 10.1 is uncertain) incorporate traditions that are to be found later in Luke's second volume, Acts. It is questionable if any of these instructions recalls actual words of Jesus: all are likely to be the experiences of those early missionaries read back as prophecies on Jesus' lips. This is not to impute dishonest motives to those who were responsible for writing up the sayings in this way. If the early missionaries had experiences such as appear in Luke 9–10 believing they were influenced by and were working for the risen Christ then they doubtless felt he must in some sense have prepared them for these experiences.

Other sayings of Jesus even if not invented were adapted to the needs of a different church. The divorce saying of Matt. 19.9 fits a Jewish background and may go back to Jesus. The same saying in Mark 10.11–12 fits Roman legal procedure and this is appropriate in a gospel written in Rome.

Many scholars between the wars analysed the gospel tradition in a way similar to the examples given above. These exegetes who became known as form critics often reached radical conclusions. Many of them argued that very few of the sayings and little of the narrative in the gospels could go back to Jesus. Their judgment was perhaps too sceptical, as they too readily credited the early communities with a creativity denied to Jesus himself. Many of the sayings attributed to Jesus in fact have a semitic ring to them which not only brands them as early but Palestinian as well. This increases the likelihood of their authenticity as words of Jesus. It must also be remembered that sayings were not indiscriminately attributed to Jesus, at least in the early days of the church. Paul in I Cor. 7 deals with various questions about marriage and is careful there to distinguish between his own pronouncements and those he received from his Lord (cf. I Cor. 7.10 and 7.12).

It is difficult nowadays to work through the gospel accounts of Jesus' ministry and to decide at each point which parts are original to Jesus and which came from the creative theological needs of the early church many years after the first Easter. From the point of view of the Christian theologian this is not necessarily important. Insofar as the earliest Christians were working within a tradition, believing themselves to be divinely inspired, it should not matter whether or not each saying attributed to Jesus in the gospels literally came from his lips directly. If the values and opinions expressed in his name came from men claiming to be his followers they need not be seen as less inspired. Such theologians need not believe that divine pronouncement ended with Jesus, but may argue that legitimate reinterpretations continued throughout the writing of the New Testament and that such reinterpretations are still being mediated through the church. Many contemporary Christians seek to justify their opinions by claiming the authority to be speaking in Christ's name. But for the historian, determined to reconstruct the life of Jesus before the faith of the post-Easter church reviewed his career and imbued his pronouncements with a spirituality previously absent, the gospels need to be examined with circumspection. As a rough rule of thumb the interests and theological and practical pre-occupations of the growing gentile church are likely to be post-Easter creations. Sayings of a semitic character set within a Jewish context and sayings that are concerned with the establishment of the kingdom of God or with the reinterpretation of the law have a stronger claim to be original to Jesus.

II

Conscious of these restrictions and difficulties it is perhaps possible nonetheless to hazard some remarks about the nature of Jesus' ministry. The duration of his independent activity is indeterminate, but it is unlikely to have lasted more than a few years. The geographical arena in which he worked was also limited. Most of his career seems to have been restricted to the Galilee. Being known as Jesus of Nazareth suggests that he spent much of his time away from that town. There are only a few geographical references given in the gospels but most are to the area around Lake Gennesaret, in locations such as Capernaum (Matt. 8.5) or Bethsaida (Mark 8.22). There are in addition stories that place Jesus in the Decapolis (Mark 7.31), Samaria (Luke 17.11; John 4.7), and in Tyre and Sidon (Mark 7.24). The synoptics do not have Jesus in Jerusalem during his ministry prior to the triumphal entry. Jerusalem is such a theologically significant place that, just as we suspected John's motives in having Jesus make several journeys there were theological, we may also suspect the synoptics' denial of any contact by Jesus with the city where he was to meet his death. Luke at 4.44, 7.17 certainly betrays a tradition that Jesus had worked and was known in Judea, even though this gospel avoids stories set in Jerusalem, before the gospel reaches its climax in chapter 19.

Jesus often travelled in the company of twelve close followers, although in some accounts of his ministry he is also attended by a wider groups of disciples. If Jesus' movement was in any sense an attempt to preach the renewal of Israel it is not improbable that he selected as his closest companions twelve men to represent and personify the twelve tribes. Matthew 19.28 speaks of the disciples each judging one of the tribes of Israel in the new world. The historicity of the calling of twelve disciples is re-enforced by the fact that, although the New Testament knows of the tradition, the lists of twelve names found in four different books (Mark 3.16–19; Matt. 10.2–4; Luke 6.14–16 and Acts 1.13) do not agree. The textual transmission of these differing names in the manuscripts shows how scribes tried to harmonize the originally discrepant lists. In fact during Jesus' ministry only the leading disciples, Peter with James and John (the sons of Zebedee), figure prominently by name and act as an inner core, taking part in certain significant events or being spokesmen for their colleagues. Certain of the twelve were remembered by the early Christians but some other names were lost in oblivion. The disciples generally and Peter in particular are written about in an unflattering way in many gospel narratives. Reasons why this should be so are to be investigated in chapter 7. It is sufficient at this point to note that the historical situation may well have been different, and the disciples, contrary to the impression created by many of the accounts in the gospels, were perceptive, loyal and fearless companions of Jesus.

Another group of people close to Jesus on his travels is his family, but, like the twelve disciples, they too are given bad publicity in the gospels. In view of the particularly distorted picture of them in the New Testament it is interesting to examine in detail what the evangelists say about Jesus' mother and his siblings. In Mark his mother is referred to but not in a favourable light. Like Paul, Mark shows no knowledge of the infancy narratives and, according to our most likely text at 6.3, refers to Jesus as 'son of the carpenter'. In the parallel to this verse in Matthew's gospel Matthew adds (13.55) that his mother's name is Mary. This is not surprising insofar as Matthew is the first gospel to mention Mary elsewhere by name. Alone among New Testament authors only Matthew and Luke refer to Jesus' mother by her name.

Not only does Mark not mention Mary by name but neither she nor Jesus' siblings play any part in Jesus' ministry. They are first referred to in Mark 3.21 where it is said they claim Jesus is mad. They are thus depicted as being equivalent to the scribes in the following story (Mark 3.22–30) who say Jesus is possessed by the devil. The composition of Mark's gospel often involved the dramatic juxtaposition of stories. The Beelzebub controversy of 3.22–30 is sandwiched by another story involving the family (3.31–35). In this episode Jesus' brothers and sisters (if one accepts the longer text here), and his mother are literally and metaphorically outsiders – they stand outside the circle of Jesus' audience unable to reach him, but he is unconcerned. Jesus is made to say here that his real family has nothing to do with heredity.

The next, and last, mention of the family is in Mark 6.1–6 which again is hostile to them. Here Jesus appears in his home town, Nazareth, but his reception is unenthusiastic. He then claims to have been rejected by his family.

Matthew, as so often, follows Mark and his retelling of the Markan stories in Matt. 12.46–50 (defining those who constitute Jesus' family) and 13.53–58 (the rejection in Nazareth) is close to Mark. Matthew however adds an account of Jesus' birth. In contrast to Luke's infancy story, Matthew's account emphasizes not Mary but Joseph. Obviously in a story of Jesus' birth his parents are necessary *dramatis personae* but taken within the context of the book as a whole neither Mary nor indeed Joseph are of any special significance.

Luke's account of Jesus' birth enhances Mary but elsewhere his picture of the family is similar to Mark's. In the stories of the ministry itself, likely to have been composed at an earlier stage than the birth story, Mary is no more sympathetically portrayed than in the earlier gospels. Indeed Luke does not name her outside chapters 1–2 preferring to call her only 'his mother'. Even the story of the rejection at Nazareth is heightened and Jesus has to escape from the congregation in his home town because they wish to kill him.

Luke defines the true family of Jesus in 8.19–21 and in this is not dissimilar to Mark. He also includes a second story with a similar message at 11.27–28 where Jesus tells the woman heckler in the crowd that he sets no store by his earthly mother. Also it is in Luke's gospel that we have that difficult saying unpopular with contemporary preachers in which Jesus is represented as refusing to accept as his followers those who do not *hate* their parents and siblings (Luke 14.26). The redefinition of the family of Jesus is thus a developing theme in the growing gospel tradition.

As far as the synoptic gospels are concerned therefore it is apparent that with the exception of the annunciation story the references to Jesus' mother and family are generally hostile. The family are of no importance for Jesus' career after the rejection at Nazareth. Indeed Joseph appears only in the birth stories.

It is only when we turn to the Fourth Gospel that the picture changes somewhat. As so often John has a different slant. Here Mary occurs in two new scenes, one at the beginning and one at the end of Jesus' ministry. The first is at the marriage feast in Cana when Jesus changes the water into wine. Mary is one of the wedding guests. In this scene Jesus addresses his mother as 'woman'. This form of address is not to be seen as implying any lack of respect but it does put her on the same level as the Samaritan woman of John 4.21 and Mary Magdalene in 20.13, 15. This would be consistent with the synoptics' picture of Jesus' family being given no special status. But it is in Jesus' further words to his mother in the Cana story that an even harsher note obtrudes. He asks her 'what do we have in common' which is virtually the same wording used by the *demoniac* to Jesus in Mark 1.24. These words which seem to fit ill with the context imply a refusal on Jesus' part to remedy the catering deficiencies to which Mary draws attention whereas the development of the story has Jesus meet his mother's request. This verse (John 2.4) therefore seems to be an anti-Mary statement inserted into the original version of the story.

In the second scene Mary is in Jerusalem at the foot of Jesus' cross. Jesus commands the 'beloved disciple', that enigmatic and anonymous character peculiar to this gospel, to care for his mother. The beloved disciple is un-named, so is his mother. (Of the fourteen occurrences of the name 'Mary' in this gospel none refers to his mother!) This story is an idealized scene – much loved by designers of rood screens – in which the disciples and the family work together after Jesus death. The disciple in the scene is called a son of Mary implying a close partnership. Such a remembrance might well be historic, as we shall see later, but it is not consistent with the picture in the gospel as a whole.

Jesus' separation from his mother and family is found in this gospel also. The statement that Jesus was dishonoured in his own country is maintained in John 4.44. We are also told in this gospel (unlike the synoptics) that Jesus paid several visits to Jerusalem for Jewish festivals (2.13; 5.1; 6.4). The Passover in particular is normally celebrated within a family context but there is no evidence that Jesus' family went with him on his Passover pilgrimages. Even though at 2.12 Jesus is accompanied by his mother and brothers in Capernaum, in the following verse Jesus alone goes to Jerusalem for Passover. At 7.5 John tells us that Jesus' brothers do not believe in him. Apparently because of this Jesus deserts them and is not accompanied by them when he goes to Jerusalem to celebrate the Feast of Tabernacles (John 7.10). The main difference in the Fourth Gospel's portrayal of Mary is therefore that she is favourably presented in the unique scene at the foot of the cross. Mary's presence in Jerusalem there is also in contrast to the synoptics' portrayal where it seems as if Mary remains in the Galilee during Jesus' ministry, although it is possible that Mary the mother of James and Joses who witnessed the crucifixion from afar in Mark 15.40 and Matthew 27.56 is Jesus' mother insofar as two of Jesus' brothers are called James and Joses according to Mark 6.3.

John's unambiguous reference to Mary's presence in Jerusalem is in accord with Acts 1.14 which tells that after Easter Mary and Jesus' brothers were staying in the city as members of the church. There is much early, and historical, material in Acts, especially in the opening chapters, despite the comparatively late date when Acts was probably composed (about AD 90). Mary herself does not reappear and we have no knowledge of her subsequent career. Tradition has it that she settled at Panaya Kapulu near Ephesus, but Luke in Acts certainly has no interest in or knowledge of her later life. Jesus' brother James however not only seems to have stayed on in Jerusalem but became leader of the church there after Peter's mysterious disappearance. Paul's letters confirm and add to the information in Acts at Galatians 1.19. In addition I Corinthians 9.5 suggests that Jesus' other brothers were also prominent in the church. By contrast Luke's general disapproval of the family evidenced in the bulk of his gospel is also apparent in his second volume in that Acts not only makes perfunctory reference to Mary but nowhere actually says that James the leader of the Jerusalem church was Jesus' brother!

If we are to assess the events discussed above chronologically then it would appear that Jesus broke with his family during his early Galilean ministry but that after his death Mary and his brothers were reconciled with the disciples and gained prominence possibly because of their claims to kinship. It is interesting to note that in the earliest list of post-resurrection appearances in I Corinthians 15.5–8 only three individuals are named, Peter (Kephas), James presumably Jesus' brother, and Paul himself. The first two are leaders respectively of the disciples and the family after Jesus' death. Paul seeks equality with them. Claims by these three to have seen the risen Jesus seem to have stood them in good stead in their respective struggles for power in the early church. Only the most important names in the church had resurrection appearances attached to them, thus James' status here is established and suggests a complete reconciliation. But this chronology and interpretation of the New Testament stories about the family causes problems.

It is unlikely that the disciples would have accepted the presence of Mary and the brothers among them in the nascent church if Jesus had in fact split from his family apparently so irrevocably. We therefore call into question the impression gained from the gospels. Another explanation is possible.

James when leader of the Jerusalem church was leader of the strictly pro-Jewish faction. This Jerusalem-based church harassed and bridled Paul's pro-gentile mission. The gospels and Acts were written by and large from the standpoint of this expansionist pro-gentile movement hence Jesus' relatives and disciples are viewed with some suspicion by the writers of the gospels. Although the gentile Christians needed to foster their links with the erstwhile companions of the earthly Jesus, both for the sake of theological continuity and social acceptability, their hostile attitude to Mary, the brothers and the disciples, all of whom were prominent in the Jerusalem-based church, has influenced the way they wrote their accounts of Jesus' ministry. Galatians 2 gives a near-contemporary impression of the hostile relationships between the two branches of Christianity. In addition, the apparent lack of success by Paul and the pro-gentile movement in evangelizing the Galilee and their consequent need to spread instead into the mediterranean area may have also coloured their attitude to the Galilee and may explain the hostile references to Nazareth and by extension to Jesus' family roots. Nazareth in particular seems to have gained a bad reputation – John 1.46 quotes a popular tag 'Can anything good come from Nazareth?'.

In contrast to the general impression given in the gospels the historical situation seems to be that Jesus was indeed close to Mary and his siblings. Clues to this effect can be found even in the gospels. Evangelists did not succeed entirely in eliminating all the historical traditions underlying their writing. 'Those around Jesus' is the way Mark describes the family in 3.21 when they say he is mad: at 4.10 a similar expression is found when it is stated that they and the twelve disciples travel together around the Galilee.

John 2.12 also suggests the family moved around in a group with the disciples and we have seen there is evidence that Mary was in Jerusalem at the time of the crucifixion. The original core of the Cana story has Jesus and his mother together in harmony. Much material concerning the family though has been omitted or falsified in the gospel accounts but Paul's letters and Acts show us that the family carried on Jesus' intentions and mission after his death.

This excursus on the family concludes that they and the disciples together with other companions, some of whom were women (Luke 8.2; 23.55), moved around together as a group more cohesive and united than is suggested by a cursory reading of the gospels but for the reasons given earlier it is difficult to determine what Jesus sought to achieve by his teaching with this group.

When he left John the Baptist's movement he seems to have set himself up as a messianic leader. Many details in the gospels state he was a Messiah: he is identified as such by the demons and the demon-possessed in Mark 1.24, 34; 5.7 and calls himself Messiah in John 4.26. Peter calls Jesus 'Messiah' at Caesarea Philippi. (However denigrated this claim was in Mark's report the confession forms the climax to the first half of Mark's gospel the title to which claims that Jesus is not only Son of God, to take the longer text at 1.1, but also the Messiah. The second title in Mark 1.1 is confessed near the end of the gospel when the centurion at the foot of the cross calls Jesus 'a', or 'the', 'son of God'.) The travellers on the road to

Emmaus in Luke 24.21 saw in Jesus one who would redeem Israel. In answer to the Baptist's question from prison asking if Jesus was in fact the one who is to come, that is the Messiah, Jesus replies positively by pointing to his miracle working (Matt. 11.5).

These and other similar references show that, despite the tendency of the evangelists to minimize Jesus' role as Messiah, there was a strong tradition that Jesus did attract publicity of such a type through his words and deeds that he was seen as a legitimate Messianic claimant.

Many of the gospels' stories tell of miraculous deeds. This was because the Messiah was identified as a miracle worker. Not only is Matt. 11.5 used to show that Jesus is indeed the one who is to come but Matt. 12.17–21 shows that miracle working fulfils Old Testament prophecies that were applied to the Messiah. From the historical point of view it is very unlikely that any of the miracles are historic. These stories were inevitable additions to the accounts of Jesus' ministry just as similar miracles were later attributed to Peter, Paul and other early Christians in Acts as they were working in imitation of Jesus. The thinking behind these stories seems to have been that if Jesus was who the Christians believed he was, then he must by definition have been able to perform miracles. Attempts to rationalize or demythologize the miracles are to be untrue to their original purpose of showing Jesus as a divinely inspired Messianic figure and thereby evoking faith in others. The miraculous element is native to these stories and is inherent in them. Jesus' nature miracles such as the walking on the water and the stilling of the storm for instance are attempts to portray Jesus as a divine figure capable of acting like Yahweh in the Old Testament. The miraculous draft of fishes and the multiplication of the loaves and fishes possibly originated in the context of the early church's eucharistic gatherings and show Jesus as the great provider, the giver of the new manna and the Messiah presiding over his banquet. The healing miracles are to be seen within the context of first-century ideas about illness and the belief that illness was the result of sin. If Jesus' movement had as one of its motives the cleansing of sin from Israel then to rid evil in the form of disease was an appropriate activity to be attributed to Jesus.

Jesus himself is unlikely to have acted as a miracle worker but once he was being proclaimed as a Son of God, risen Lord and

Messianic saviour by the early Christians then it was inevitable that miraculous events would be added to his life story. The miracle stories are therefore to be seen as theological statements in dramatized form.

The extent to which Jesus himself was responsible for encouraging others to see him as Messiah is uncertain because the evangelists have doctored the tradition. In several places the gospels imply that Jesus refused to be described as Messiah, for instance at Mark 1.25, 34; 5.43. Many scholars argue that these attempts to silence affirmations of Messiahship in the gospels are editorial. Mark in particular seems to have imposed on the material a messianic secrecy at least in the Galilean stories. This is significant. Mark's gospel is likely to have had a Roman provenance. Given the opprobrium which the title Messiah attracted it is not surprising that Mark plays down any suggestion that Jesus was a traditional or political Messiah. His death as a messianic king is attributed to malevolence on the part of the Jews. In order to promote Christianity as posing no threat to the Roman state not only are the Roman authorities during the trial presented in a favourable light, but Jesus' messiahship is either underplayed or reinterpreted. Hence Jesus is said to accept as a title for himself the innocent 'Son of Man' rather than the politically explosive title 'Messiah'. The title Messiah then became little more than a proper name once Christianity spread.

There is however sufficient evidence in the gospels to suggest that despite the attempts by the evangelists to modify or reduce the messianic role played by Jesus he did in fact set out to be the Messiah and he was correctly seen as such by the crowds. The anointing at Bethany which made him the kingly Messiah or 'anointed one', the triumphal entry into Jerusalem when Jesus incongruously rides in seated on two animals simultaneously according to Matt. 21.2–7 with its literalist interpretation of the Messianic prophecy of Zech. 9.9, the acclaim by the crowds of him as the one who is to come, and the attempt by Jesus forcibly to apply in the temple principles enunciated in his ministry, all present a tradition of Jesus consciously fulfilling messianic expectations.

But as the Messiah Jesus seems to have been more than the mere political figure, which previous messiahs tended to be. Many of the sayings attributed to Jesus place him firmly in the tradition inaugurated by John the Baptist as the moral restorer of Israel. As such he set out to reinterpret Jewish tradition and the Law. It is likely that many sayings in which Jesus rigorously and puritanically reinterprets the Mosaic Law are original, for example in Matt. 5.17–48; 23; Mark 10.17–22, although the dramatized story known as the transfiguration in Mark 9.2–8 when Jesus supersedes the law, personified by Moses, and the prophets, represented by Elijah is secondary. This latter goes beyond the stories when Jesus merely reinterprets the law and as such the transfiguration with its pro-Pauline bias is unlikely to represent Jesus' own aims. Far from abolishing the law and prophets Jesus seems to have attempted to fulfil them rigorously.

The reason why Jesus' movement tried to purify Israel was because of its belief in the imminent coming of the kingdom of God. This kingdom was possibly eschatological but partly it was political. Although some of Jesus' followers interpreted it as exclusively political it was also a religious movement. This aspect of Jesus' work is often neglected by those who describe Jesus only as a type of Zealot leader, just as the political dimension of his role is often ignored by theologians who like the evangelists before them are intent on promoting Jesus as a pacific saviour.

Rabbinic sayings which do not contain any pro-Pauline sentiment are likely to be authentic to Jesus. So too are the bulk of the parables. These homely folk-tales have a distinctive character and poignancy. Many of them are similar in style and background and they demand a common origin. It is therefore not impossible that the majority of the parables, especially the parables of the kingdom, originated with Jesus. In them the imminence of the kingdom of God is proclaimed. This belief was the main motive behind Jesus' preaching and actions insofar as he saw himself as possessing an active and influential role in bringing this kingdom into being. This would explain why he demanded a religious revival and moral adjustment on the part of his co-religionists. Stories and sayings that fit this pattern are likely to represent the earliest strand of the tradition. Stories and sayings that impute divinity and divine status to Jesus or which minimize his messiahship or his pro-Jewishness are likely to be secondary, reflecting the interests, beliefs and presuppositions of the post-Easter and Pauline dominated churches.

Jesus' mission seems to have been directed primarily at Jews. Stories and sayings that imply a universalist mission also reflect post-Easter traditions. Those difficult sayings in which Jesus states that his mission is to Jews only and those stories in which Jesus is represented as only reluctantly accepting such as the Syro-Phoenician woman into his movement are likely to show the original purpose of his preaching. The gentile missionary activities of the early Christians created much dissent within the church: had Jesus intended his message to be spread in this way then it is improbable that Paul and his companions would have found their gentile mission thwarted on so many occasions by Jewish Christians.

It is doubtful if Jesus ever anticipated founding a church at all although later Christians assumed he intended founding both a permanent movement and a cultus. In so far as the meal Jesus shared with his disciples on the night he was arrested turned out to be the last such supper, that meal inevitably was imbued with especial significance by his erstwhile companions. The instruction attributed to Jesus that the meal was to be regarded as a memorial to him is to be seen as an ecclesiastical reading back into Jesus' life the post-Easter practice of the church. The concluding words of Jesus in Matthew's gospel with their anachronistic trinitarian formula (Matt. 28.19) anticipating a world-wide mission also represent not the intention of Jesus but the practices of that branch of the church which produced this gospel. The establishment of Peter as founder of the church in Matt. 16 and the instructions given to the apostolic mission in Luke 9–10 are likewise *vaticinia ex eventu*.

Jesus is unlikely to have anticipated his movement's continuing beyond his death. The passion predictions placed on his lips contain prophecies of his death and resurrection. These too are prophecies after the event. It is unlikely that Jesus expected his triumphal entry to Jerusalem to result in failure and death. It is even less likely that he expected his aims to be carried out only after his death. It is probable that he expected to establish, or at least prepare Judaism for, the kingdom of God during his lifetime with his family, disciples and other followers as the initial group of those so prepared. His eschatological pronouncements over Jerusalem and its temple encouraged those who entered Jerusalem triumphantly with him to expect this visit to inaugurate the new age. This expectation failed and it was only after Jesus' death that his former colleagues and the family reconsidered his role and in the belief that Jesus was raised from the dead and was still guiding them, they reassembled to fight for his ideals.

The popularity of Jesus' arrival in Jerusalem like his success in the Galilee is likely to represent the historical situation. However congenial such reports would be to the evangelists it is evident that the reaction of the Romans to Jesus, his death and the subsequent continuation of his movement demanded a figure of significance and stature. Jesus' authority is a constant feature of the gospels. This and his self-consciousness brand him as a man of influence. His evident power, popularity and charisma are the starting points for subsequent elaboration of his role.

The reinterpretation of Jesus' role necessitated by an attempt to avoid overt messianism resulted in Jesus' being described as a divine figure. The nature miracles which possibly began as proofs of mere messiahship encouraged the divinization of Jesus in the minds of the earliest Christians. Despite the inherent reserve of monotheistic writers, the evangelists nevertheless equated Jesus with God, attributing to him titles and functions which in the Old Testament are reserved for God. The ambiguous title 'Lord' comes to be used even of the earthly Jesus. Statements such as 'I and the Father are one' are placed with some regularity on Jesus' lips by John (cf. John 10.37–38; 1.1, 18).

Jesus the Messiah and religious reformer was gradually transformed to Jesus the risen Lord leading his erstwhile colleagues after his death. The one who proclaims the message in his ministry became the one who was proclaimed after his death. But the ministry was written about by those who believed in him as a divine saviour and this creates the dilemma for historians wishing to separate from the gospels material which pre-dates Jesus' death. After the resurrection Jesus the Messiah and peripatetic preacher of the kingdom of God was obviously seen in a new light once it was believed that Jesus had survived death and had already entered into the realm of God: all that he said and did prior to his death was obviously reinterpreted as having happened to a divine figure destined for immortality. Hence the elusiveness of the historic Jesus and the numerous quests for the pre-Easter beliefs of Jesus and his movement.

Texts

Jesus' ministry is covered in Mark 1–13, Matt. 3–20, Luke 3–22, John 1–17. A suitable sample which might illustrate many of the points in the chapter would be either Mark 2.1–3.6 or Luke 6.

Bibliography

M. Black, *An Aramaic Approach to the Gospels and Acts*, Clarendon Press, 3rd ed. 1967; R. Bultmann, *The History of the Synoptic Tradition* Blackwell 1963; H. Conzelmann, *An Outline of the Theology of the New Testament*, SCM Press 1969; J. Jeremias, *The Parables of Jesus*, SCM Press 6th ed. 1963; I. H. Marshall, *The Gospel of Luke*, Paternoster 1978; D. Nineham, *Saint Mark*, Penguin Books 1963; E. Schillebeeckx, *Jesus: An Experiment in Christology*, Collins 1979; W. Wrede, *The Messianic Secret*, J. Clarke 1971.

4 The Trials and Death of Jesus

The importance of the trials and death of Jesus for the early church is undeniable. The New Testament writers were interested in the events leading up to Jesus' death but these events created two problems. First the earliest Christians needed to explain why and how Jesus was killed by the Romans. Secondly the early theologians of the church, determined to promote Jesus as the new Jewish saviour, had the task of explaining why it was necessary for Jesus the Jew to become anathema to the Jews by being crucified. The Jewish Law (Deut. 21.23) stated that God cursed those who were 'hanged on a tree'. This was made to include crucifixion in Roman times. Paul for instance is much concerned with this theological paradox especially in Galatians and in Romans. For the gospel writers, however, it was the first problem that exercised them more.

The crucifixion became an essential part of Christian theology not just for its own sake but because it was linked irrevocably with the raising of Jesus from the dead. It is on this belief in Jesus' resurrection that the distinctly Christian message of life and hope in eternal salvation is based. The raising of Jesus presupposes, and needs, his actual death and burial at one point in history. In that sense the story of the crucifixion is subordinate to the resurrection in Christian theology. Each gospel reaches its climax with its concluding proclamation of the resurrection. The trials and crucifixion needed to be explained but only within the wider context of the Christian belief about Jesus' ultimate significance. The resurrection message is dependent on the burial story; and the burial is dependent on his death. Thus the evangelists had to relate how Jesus met his end.

The passion story in all four gospels relates how Jesus having entered Jerusalem in triumph is subsequently arrested in Geth-semane. Between them the evangelists relate three separate trials that Jesus underwent, one before the leaders of the Jews, one before King Herod, and the decisive trial before Pontius Pilate, the Roman Governor, that led to his being crucified.

I

Two questions come to mind whenever the crucifixion of Jesus is considered. These are 'Why was Jesus killed?' and 'With what justification did he suffer a Roman punishment?'. Crucifixion meant that Jesus must have committed a crime against the Roman state. Had he merely offended against a technicality in the Jewish law then it is likely he could have been punished by Jews. It will be argued below that even during the Roman occupation the Jews did have the right to exercise the death penalty and that statements to the contrary in the New Testament are apologetically motivated.

The most plausible answer to the first question above is found in those sections of the passion story which say Jesus was killed as a political aspirant. The Fourth Gospel implies, probably correctly, that a Roman cohort was involved in arresting Jesus (John 18.3, 12) which suggests Jesus was sought as an enemy of Rome. The gospels also state, again probably correctly, that Jesus died as a king: the superscription on the cross that Jesus was seen as 'King of the Jews' is in effect the correct judgment. The Romans could well have been interested in Jesus if he were identified as a king, and they could have executed any such aspirant at a time of political unrest. An interest-ing sidelight on the contemporary political situation is found in John 11.48. Here the chief priests and the Pharisees are concerned that if they allow Jesus free rein to act as a political Messiah, the Romans will destroy the temple and the nation. This statement written by John after the Romans had in fact destroyed the temple and Jeru-salem in AD 70 is clearly ironic: the Jews did not leave Jesus alone yet they still suffered loss. The context of this saying is the raising of Lazarus and the aftermath, but it highlights the contemporary situation in which the Romans would be interested in quelling a political aspirant. Performing such miracles as John records would be interpreted at that time as messianic.

The extent to which Jesus saw himself as a political king or as a rival to Caesar as his prosecution alleged is difficult to determine. The self-consciousness of Jesus cannot easily be recovered from the gospels, but if the triumphal entry recalls an actual event, then Jesus did indeed enact a messianic prophecy by entering Jerusalem as king of the Jews, and, as the story is told, the event seems to have been carefully rehearsed and elaborately planned beforehand. Another consideration relevant to this question is that as Jesus' mission in life seems to have been to establish the kingdom of God then such a purpose would inevitably imply the overthrow or abolition of the existing world order. Possibly Jesus' motive was purely otherworldly and eschatological but certainly such an aim must have encouraged his hearers to see in him the new Davidic king and messiah, who would in fact restore the kingdom of God on earth. The men walking to Emmaus in Luke 24.21 are represented as interpreting Jesus' ministry in this way, and the crowds at the triumphal entry in John 12.13 wave their palms of victory indicating that they saw Jesus' arrival as a coronation procession. The same point is made in the synoptic gospels' telling that garments were spread in Jesus' path just as they were for the Old Testament kings like Jehu (II Kings 9.13) during their coronation procession. At this procession Jesus is hailed as King of Israel: John and Luke in fact add the words 'King of Israel' and 'King' respectively to Psalm 118.26 quoted in all four gospels. At this point in the narrative Jesus' popularity with the Jewish crowds in Jerusalem is as great as it is said to have been in his earlier Galilean ministry. The subsequent hostility shown by the Jews as a whole during the trial and crucifixion is likely to reflect not so much a change in the Jewish attitude to Jesus during that week in Jerusalem, but a change imposed on the material by the evangelists. The gospel writers' determination to make the Jews the enemies of Jesus both during the trial and at earlier points in his ministry is because they wished to read back contemporary attitudes in the early church into the life of Jesus himself. Those traditions which preserve the general popularity and acclaim of Jesus by the Jewish crowds are probably historic. He was hailed as a king and messiah by his contemporaries, even though the gospel writers had of necessity to redefine these terms by universalizing them and making them seem politically neutral.

John's gospel for example has Jesus define the nature of his kingship. In the trial before Pilate this is particularly marked. In contrast to the silent Jesus of the other gospels at this point, the Fourth Gospel has Jesus give Pilate a lesson in Johannine theology and in so doing explains his kingship as otherworldly. Such an explanation was obviously necessary in a church determined to show Jesus – and, by extension, all Christians – as no threat to the Roman state. This purpose may also be seen in I Peter 2.13–16.

A similar purpose lies behind the saying of the tribute money. The charge by the prosecution in Luke 23.2 is that Jesus forbade the paying of tribute to Rome. Jesus' actual statement about tribute money appears earlier in the gospels: 'Render unto Caesar the things that are Caesar's and to God what is God's.' Such a pronouncement was of crucial importance to the early church confronted by authorities determined to test the attitude of Christians towards the state and the saying as recorded in the gospels (Mark 12.17 and parallels) is evidently intended to show that religious and civic duty do not clash, although if the saying does indeed go back to Jesus such a sentiment may well have been intended to have the opposite effect, namely that Israel was God's and not Caesar's hence Caesar had no right to claim taxes from Jews living there. If this interpretation is correct, the prosecution may have been making a sound case.

There are in addition to that saying, other statements by Jesus, which appear uncharacteristic of the normal image of Jesus projected in the New Testament as a whole. These include those sayings which state that Jesus' mission was to set men at variance with other men, and that he has come not to bring peace but a sword (Matt. 10.34–35). An incongruous event comparable with these uncharacteristic sayings occurs in the Gethsemane story. The New Testament tells that the disciples were armed with at least two swords (Luke 22.38) and that during Jesus' arrest one man, the high priest's servant, was injured and his ear evulsed. As that tradition developed names were, as usual, added to the nameless: the swordsman becomes Peter and the high priest's servant is named as Malchus by John. Other details were added: the ear becomes the more significant right ear and Luke characteristically turns the affray into a healing miracle thereby distracting his readers from the original episode.

Another story that seems to have been adjusted in order to deflect the reader from its original and historical context is the anointing story. Historically the anointing of Jesus in Bethany prior to the triumphal entry (according to the chronology on the Fourth Gospel) was likely to have been the occasion when Jesus was publicly anointed as King-Messiah. The evangelists' embarrassment at this coronation is evidence in the later accounts of Luke and John when Jesus is anointed not as a king was (on the head) as Matthew and Mark say, but on the feet, and also in the varying interpretations given by Jesus of the anointer's motive and purpose that are written into each of the four evangelists' accounts of this story (Mark 14.3–9 and parallels). That the crowds wished to have Jesus anointed as king is evidenced also at John 6.15 which tells how Jesus had to escape to prevent this happening. There is a constant attempt by the evangelist to tone down such references in the tradition to Jesus as Messiah (or anointed one) and as a consecrated king. This is especially evident in Mark's gospel which seems to impose a secrecy over Jesus' messianic doings and sayings – especially in those stories having a Galilean context.

Other indications in the gospels that suggest the Roman trial was based on reliable evidence are that Jesus' colleagues appear to have been the sort of people likely to alarm the Roman authorities. At least one of the disciples seems to have been an extreme nationalist: this is Simon the Zealot (Luke 6.15; Acts 1.13) whom Matthew and Mark knew only by the 'safer' name Simon the Cananaean. Other disciples include the 'sons of thunder' (Mark 3.17 only), and Judas Iscariot, whose second name has been interpreted by some scholars as meaning 'assassin'. It is not surprising therefore that the authorities who arrest Jesus are said by him in all the synoptic gospels to have come prepared to arrest a Zealot.

The above considerations, together with the saying about the destruction of the temple (which will be considered fully below) show that Jesus' movement was not as pacific as the evangelists generally wished to suggest. It may well be that such sayings and actions as these did lead to his arrest. But to suggest that these sayings and actions were the only aspects of Jesus' mission original to him is to distort the picture and to misinterpret Jesus' motives identifying these with his methods. Jesus was remembered and later worshipped as a religious leader and saviour not as an insurrectionist. His erstwhile colleagues and subsequent generations of Christians underplayed or overlooked the violence in Jesus' career and concentrated on his wider teaching much of which is as likely to proceed from the historic Jesus as the 'violent sayings' identified above.

Care needs to be taken in interpreting Jesus' culpability in Roman eyes. Those modern authors who have tried to portray Jesus as an exclusively political being are as biased as the evangelists who were trying to dismiss or deny any political role for Jesus. As a religious reformer determined to purify Israel he must have been political, yet those commentators who stress only the violent acts and sayings in order to recruit Jesus for the fashionably socialistic cause of political activism are distorting the New Testament picture understood as a totality.

II

Even in New Testament times the interpretation and recording of Jesus' trials and death needed careful handling. The early church was scrupulous in avoiding confrontation with the Roman authorities and attempted to conduct itself in such a way as not to anger the Romans. This care has already been indicated in the passage about tribute payment above. Even greater readjustment was needed in the passion narrative, insofar as Roman involvement in the judicial process could not be avoided. In other parts of the New Testament where the trials are not recorded the need to face this issue does not arise. In the early speeches in Acts it is the Jews who are accused of the death. Peter speaking to the men of Judea and Jerusalem in Acts 2 tells them *they* have crucified Jesus (2.23, 36). At Acts 4.10 Peter speaking to the rulers and elders of Israel delivers a similar message. In Acts 5.30 Peter and the other apostles accuse the Sanhedrin and the high priest of 'hanging Jesus on a tree'.

The emphasis in these speeches is not on the trial or even the death but on the subsequent resurrection of Jesus. These speeches probably represent the sort of teaching that the author believed the earliest preachers gave. There is a slight development in Acts 13.27–31 in a speech attributed to Paul, insofar as Pilate is referred to. It is said there that he was forced by the Jews to have Jesus killed, but again the trial is not referred to.

When the gospels were written, however, from an ostensibly historical standpoint as a chronicle of the events of Jesus' trial and death, the crucifixion had to be explained. Crucifixion though was known to be a Roman form of capital punishment, and at the time the gospels were written, the church was dependent to a large degree on the tacit support and approval of the Roman authorities. Mark's gospel for instance was possibly written in Rome itself. Missionaries in the early church were aware that as they increased their activities in the Roman Empire and established an increasingly significant religious movement, the goodwill of the governing authorities was of paramount importance. Paul himself in his epistle to Rome significantly states not only that his hearers must obey the civil government but also that 'all governors are instituted by God' (Rom. 13. 1–4).

Any opposition to Paul referred to in his letters, or any opposition to the Christians in Acts, seems to have come not from the Romans but from the Judaizers or Jewish Christians. If there were any brushes with the Roman authorities Acts is careful to underplay them. Similarly in the gospels, opposition to Jesus' teaching and actions during the whole of his ministry comes from Jews, who are pictured as constantly lurking and waiting to attack him. There is no contact with the Roman authorities until the trial before Pilate. Hence the embarrassment when that trial has to be described.

Although Acts shows that the early speeches, which contain much material that predates the composition of the gospels, conveniently ignore the obvious part that the Romans must have played in the death of Jesus by crucifixion, this could not be the case in the gospels. The usual and normal way there of explaining how and why the new saviour Jesus Christ of Nazareth was put to death by a Roman form of punishment was to show the Roman authorities merely as the constitutional instruments obliged to put Jesus to death because of the wickedness of the Jews. The more the evangelists exonerate the Romans from the blame for Jesus' death, the more the Jews are blamed. The increasing whitewashing of Pilate and the Romans became more pronounced as the gospel tradition developed, but even in Mark's gospel, the earliest written account we have, Pilate and the Romans are presented as puppets in the hands of the Jewish mob. Throughout Mark's gospel in fact the opponents of Jesus are always the Jews: they are thus presented as the enemies of Jesus *ab initio*. Even as early as Mark 3, the Jews are plotting to destroy him.

Thereafter opposition to Jesus comes constantly from various Jewish groups such as the Pharisees or the Sadducees.

This enmity reaches its culmination in the trial narratives. The early hostility is an anticipation of the climax in the crucifixion. The gospels saw the preceding events in Jesus' life as but a prelude for his death, and resurrection. That is why the last days in Jesus' life are given so much prominence. When we read the New Testament accounts of the trials, it must be remembered that these too were written from the same standpoint as the rest of the gospel story. The trials are not court transcriptions but descriptions of how Jesus' passion was interpreted. The significance of the trial, and not its legalistic importance was what mattered to the earliest preachers.

There are several ways in which Pilate's (and by extension, the Romans') involvement with Jesus is described. In Mark Pilate is shown to be conscious of Jesus' innocence, and is said to be aware that the chief priests have handed over Jesus merely out of envy. When that tradition was elaborated by Matthew, he added the detail that Pilate's wife dreamed of Jesus' innocence. Dreams, as so often in the Bible are the means whereby divine announcements are communicated. In addition, Pilate himself dramatizes his conviction that Jesus is innocent by washing his hands of Jesus' guiltless blood. This is a poignant symbol of his non-involvement but such ritual hand-washing was in fact a Jewish not a Roman gesture (Deut. 21.6–7; Ps. 73.13). We may therefore suspect the historicity of Pilate's gesture. Those wishing to defend the accuracy of Matthew's statement may well say that Pilate was here copying a Jewish gesture in order to perform something meaningful to his audience, but it is more likely that the incident is a dramatic invention on Matthew's part – especially as Pilate is made to quote the Jewish scriptures while washing (Ps. 26.6). The juxtaposition of Pilate's innocence and Jewish guilt is particularly pronounced in this incident insofar as Pilate's statement of innocence is paralleled by the Jewish acceptance of the guilt. The words that have had such fateful consequences for Jews through the centuries 'His blood be on us and on our children' are what Matthew makes all the Jews shout out in unison thus ensuring for the race the apportionment of blame. This quotation in fact echoes and has probably been based on II Samuel 1.16 where David says to one who has killed the Lord's anointed, that is a Christ, 'Your blood be on your head'.

Luke has Pilate declare Jesus innocent three times (always a significant number in the New Testament if we compare the temptations, Peter's denial or Jesus' prayers in Gethsemane). Pilate then surrenders Jesus to the crowds' will (Luke 23.25). The crowd in Luke includes not just the Jewish leaders but 'the people', that is the whole nation (Luke 23.13). Luke alone of the evangelists even has Jesus forgive the Romans (23.34) because they are ignorant of their action. Likewise Luke has a gentile, a Roman soldier, emphasize Jesus' innocence at the time of his death. The centurian at the foot of the cross in Matthew and Mark identifies Jesus as a son of God but Luke alters these words and has the man underline the constant theme of Jesus' guiltlessness. Luke even omits any scene of mockery by the Romans; only the Jewish troops in Herod's command mock him, as indeed do those Jews holding Jesus overnight before the Sanhedrin trial.

John like Luke states that Pilate 'handed Jesus over to them to be crucified' (19.16) not necessarily implying that the Jews in fact did the crucifying, which would have been a nonsense, but that this judgment was demanded by them. That is why the words 'to them' in the sense 'to their will' are added by John to the parallel text in Matthew and Mark. In the story of the trial itself earlier in the Fourth Gospel, John has Pilate make a constitutional error. He tells the Jews to judge Jesus according to their own laws. It is strange that a Roman magistrate would give such an instruction to a subject people who had delivered a prisoner into his charge with an offence they refused to specify. It is even stranger that the subject people bandy words with Pilate, and more particularly that they should have to remind him of his constitutional position by saying that they are not allowed by the Romans to exercise the death penalty. Whether this was in fact the legal position (and authorities on Roman law in the first century are divided on this question), it was obviously of apologetic significance to John to explain the Roman involvement in Jesus' case as their reluctant acceptance of the *status quo*. Pilate thus became the constitutional instrument whereby the wicked Jews are able to exercise their will. In fact the Jews did seem able to execute those whose offence was Jewish but for the Fourth Gospel to state that the Jews were constitutionally and legally unable to do so is a convenient way of re-enforcing Pilate's innocence. In the exchange between Pilate and Jesus written into John 19.11 Jesus is made to tell Pilate that he is merely fulfilling the divine plan in sentencing Jesus and that it is the Jews who are most to blame. This explanation given by Jesus obviously reflects the dilemma the evangelists' contemporaries felt about the relative power of Jesus and Pilate at the time of the trial and at the moment of the sentencing.

Many other details in the trial story also serve this apologetic end, and account for many of the discrepencies and problems raised by the passion narrative as a whole. The trial before the Sanhedrin in particular creates many difficulties. It is unlikely that a plenary session of the Sanhedrin as recounted by Matthew and Mark would have taken place on the night of the Passover, according to the synoptic gospels' timetable. Luke, perhaps because he recognized such a difficulty, has the Sanhedrin trial in the morning prior to the Roman trial. The Fourth Gospel has no mention of the Sanhedrin trial at all, and replaces it with a few questions from the High Priest while Jesus is under house arrest during the night before his trial before Pilate.

Apart from the difficulty over the timing, the Sanhedrin trial itself is problematic. False evidence about Jesus is trumped up but is not accepted because of lack of agreement, and a second charge is brought. In fact the allegedly false charge that Jesus is reported to have said he would destroy the temple is not 'false' insofar as such words appear on Jesus' lips at Mark 13.2 when Jesus predicts the downfall of the temple. At Acts 6.14 Stephen is accused of preaching that Jesus of Nazareth would destroy the temple: this too shows that such a tradition was alive. One can only deduce that the saying is in the Sanhedrin trial only because the evangelist wanted to kill the tradition that Jesus ever said such a thing. The implication is that Jesus did indeed make such a prediction. Certainly such a sentiment would fit in with the incident of Jesus' overthrowing the money-changers' tables in the temple. But whereas the earlier accounts state such a tradition is false, the Fourth Gospel has Jesus predict the destruction of the temple but then has him reinterpret this in the light of his hearers' confusion by saying that this is not to be taken literally as he is referring to the 'temple of his body' which will rise again after three days. The original saying was obviously embarrassing to a church determined to project a pacific image. Thus they found differing ways of coping with this well-known tradition either by saying it was a false rumour put about by Jews or by reinterpreting it in a mystical way.

The next question at the Sanhedrin trial concerns Jesus' Messiahship. It is his answer to this which leads to the demand for his death as a blasphemer. As such Jesus is accused of falling foul of the Mosaic Law, but the sentence of death by stoning prescribed for such an offence in Leviticus 24.16 is not acted upon. Above it was suggested that the statement in John 18.31 that the Jews could not carry out such a sentence was apologetic and did not in fact represent the true state of affairs at that time in Palestine. The case of Stephen's stoning in Acts proves that such a death was capable of being inflicted by Jews. Also an attempt by Jesus himself to escape death by stoning is recorded in John 8.59 suggesting that here at least the writer felt he was recording the *status quo*. The same is probably true of John 7.1.

The charge presented later by the Sanhedrin to the Romans at Luke 23.2 is that Jesus was setting himself up as a king. Such an offence is more likely to have been correct in view of the subsequent events, but it is hardly the decision reached at the Sanhedrin trial itself. In fact the Sanhedrin trial as such is unlikely to have occurred either overnight or in the morning. The consistent policy running through the gospels of whitewashing Pilate has resulted in the evangelists' creating a Jewish trial parallel to the Roman, and actual, trial. This has the effect of blunting the significance of the second trial with the Roman interrogation of Jesus. The Jewish trial is likely to have been modelled on the account of the trial before Pilate and this would explain many of the doublets in the two trials. For example the silence of Jesus before his accusers occurs in both trials (Mark 14.60–61 parallels 15.5) and Jesus is mocked after both interrogations (Mark 14.65 parallels 15.17f.). This Jewish trial is anticipated earlier in the gospels: the passion predictions, especially in Matthew and Mark which are the gospels that make most of the Sanhedrin trial, refer to Jesus' being led before the chief priests and scribes and being sentenced to death (Matt. 20.18; Mark 10.33).

There were however other ways of whitewashing Pilate and the Romans, and of blaming the Jews.

In Luke for instance we read of a third trial, this one before Herod, which is introduced for a similar purpose to the Sanhedrin trial. Here again, Pilate is seen to be doing his best not to have to pass sentence. The quasi-Jewish king, Herod, like the Sanhedrin, tries Jesus in front of the vehement Jewish leaders but on this occasion no decision is reached. The episode succeeded in showing that Jesus is tried not only in front of governors like Pilate but also kings like Herod as the apostles later are to be, according to Jesus' prophecy two chapters earlier (Luke 21.12). Luke has the prophecy fulfilled not only here in Jesus' career but also in the careers of the apostles imitating Christ. In Acts 4.26 the Old Testament passage in Psalm 2.2: 'The Kings of the earth stood up and the rulers were gathered together against the Lord and against his anointed (Christ)' is quoted. This passage had therefore to be literally fulfilled in one trial for Jesus before a king and another before a ruler. Luke therefore provided these and refers to both trials in Acts 4.27.

As well as introducing Herod for the purpose of deflecting interest from Pilate, another character appears in the trial story for a similar purpose. This is Barabbas, and the references to him also cause problems. Matthew and Mark tell us (Matt. 27.15 and Mark 15.6–8) that the Roman governor was obliged to release a prisoner at the Passover. The Fourth Gospel has Pilate improbably remind the Jews that such a practice was a Jewish tradition. There is no external evidence that such a habit ever existed or that the Romans ever permitted such a custom. It is particularly strange that, as the story is told, Pilate is willing to release any prisoner the crowd wished, but then limits the amnesty to either Jesus or Barabbas, especially as at least two other criminals were available, that is the two convicts crucified alongside Jesus. It is even more remarkable, and unlikely, that Pilate would have agreed to the releasing of a dangerous murderer at a time of insurrection.

One is again left with the inevitable conclusion that the scene with Barabbas is yet another way of exonerating Pilate. The Jews choose the murderer while it is Pilate who recognizes Jesus' innocence.

The origin of the Barabbas episode is obscure. Barabbas' name is however known throughout the gospel tradition although Luke, and particularly John, make less of this incident than the other evangelists. There is no obvious scriptural passage that caused the addition of such an incident or such a character as Barabbas. One may possibly argue that there was some historical justification for Pilate's confusion over two of the prisoners brought to him. Many manuscripts in Matthew's gospel refer to Barabbas as Jesus Barabbas at 27.16, 17. These manuscripts are possibly correct: scribes would be more inclined to omit an original 'Jesus' as a name for Barabbas, once 'Jesus' was a name reserved for *the* one Jesus Christ, than to add such a sacred name to a text which read only 'Barabbas'. Most Jewish names were built up from a personal name followed by the father's name. Matthew, as is not surprising for the most Jewish in tone of the four gospels, is more scrupulous in his usage. He refers for instance to Simon Barjona at 16.17 and Zachariah Barachias at 23.35. It is less usual to refer to a man only by his patronym, although some parts of the New Testament do allow this, Joseph Barnabas for instance in Acts 4.36 is known thereafter only by his patronym. Hence 'Barabbas' is less likely to belong to the original tradition than 'Jesus Barabbas'. The whole Barabbas episode may therefore go back to a tradition that Pilate was confronted by two men named Jesus, Jesus of Nazareth and Jesus Barabbas and was confused about which one was being spoken of during the trial, especially if both were messianic claimants: the name Barabbas may in fact mean 'Son of the Father (God)'. One man was released, the other Jesus crucified.

But whatever the historical situation, if any, that gave rise to the story, the episode was used, as so many other details were, to serve the general purpose of exonerating the Romans and blaming the Jews.

This apologetic motif running through so many incidents makes us doubt the historical value of much in the stories of the trials. In addition, the speed with which all these trials are said to have been carried out strains our credulity. The whole of the passion week is in fact written with frequent indications of the passing time. In sharp contrast to the rest of Jesus' ministry where time scales and time indications are generally absent, in the passion narrative the precise happenings on each day are recorded and by the time the crucifixion takes place we are given three-hourly time checks. The whole week is breathlessly overcharged with events, meetings and teachings. It is difficult to reconstruct the likeliest timetable for Jesus' final days in Jerusalem, but, if all the events that are said to have happened actually took place then it is obvious that the evangelists have artificially telescoped them into a shorter period than was the case historically. So far as the trials are concerned these in particular have been compressed into an improbably short period. The Fourth Gospel might give us a clue that Jesus had been in Jerusalem longer than the two days suggested in Mark insofar as John 18.2 says the disciples *often* met with Jesus in the Garden of Gethsemane.

Chronology however was not the dominant concern of the evangelists. For them the main purpose of the passion story in general and the trials in particular was to whitewash Pilate. This process of exonerating Pilate continued beyond New Testament times and reached its inevitable culmination when the church in Ethiopia canonized him! The Christian picture of Pilate that originated in the trials story is of a weak and vacillating governor who is swayed by the mob. This picture is, however, at variance with descriptions of Pilate in the writings of Josephus and in the New Testament outside the trials narrative. In fact the only reference to Pilate outside the passion story is at Luke 13.1 where Pilate appears in his true historical colours as a ruthless despot. Unlike the account of the trials Luke has here left the tradition untouched.

III

Another dominant theme running through the passion narrative is the fulfilment of Old Testament passages. The place of Old Testament prophecy was paramount in the telling of Jesus' whole career. In Matthew's gospel particularly this was of especial significance. In the birth narratives much is said to happen as a result of fulfilling the Old Testament such as the birth in Bethlehem, the virgin birth, the massacre of the innocents, the call from Egypt and the Nazareth home for Jesus. There are examples in the rest of this gospel too. It is reported that Jesus preaches in the Galilee (4.15) to fulfil a passage in Isaiah; he heals (8.17) also to fulfil Isaiah and he preaches in parables (13.35) to fulfil Psalm 78. Thus, to be consistent, Jesus' death and resurrection from the dead also had to be in fulfilment of the scriptures.

The problem here was that no obvious or ready-made messianic proof-texts were available to our authors. The first-century ideas of messiah were generally of a triumphant figure. A suffering messiah was a contradiction in terms, yet, for the Christians, Jesus *was* killed and was also identified as messiah. This paradox had to be explained. The earliest Christians clearly had to justify the event and they tried to do so in their usual manner by pointing to Old Testament passages which seemed to predict what happened to Jesus at the end. I Peter 1.10 shows that the Old Testament was interpreted as anticipating the allegedly salvific events in Jesus' life. This process can also be seen at work in two passages relating to the risen Jesus. At Luke 24.25-27, in the story of the walk to Emmaus, the resurrected Jesus explains to Cleopas and his travelling companion that his death and resurrection were foretold in the Old Testament. Likewise at Luke 24.45-46 Jesus speaks in a similar way to the disciples. What the earliest apologists needed to do was to point to specific verses in the Old Testament which would illustrate this belief.

The results of this searching in the scriptures can be seen in the gospels' passion narrative. This story as a whole can be seen as a florilegium of Old Testament quotations and allusions although sometimes no specific biblical passage is in mind, as for instance when Mark 14.49 has Jesus allow himself to be arrested to fulfil what was believed to be the general purpose of the scriptures. This attitude is similar to the earlier statement by Paul in I Corinthians 15.3 that Jesus' death (as well as his burial and resurrection) are fulfilments of the Old Testament as a whole. Usually though the New Testament authors had specific passages in mind. The most significant section of the Old Testament proved to be the so-called suffering servant songs in Deutero-Isaiah (Isa. 40-55). These chapters tell of a righteous man who suffers for the guilty and whose ultimate vocation was death. This servant figure was alighted on by the early Christians to provide a biblical predecessor for Jesus. In the primitive speeches in the early chapters of Acts Jesus is referred to as a servant (Acts 3.13, 26; 4.27, 30). The search of the scriptures referred to in I Peter 1.10-11 results in the references to the suffering servant of Isaiah in I Peter 2.21-23. In the synoptic gospels' passion story the reference to Jesus' being silent at his trials is also probably an echo of Isaiah 53.7 which refers to the silence of the suffering servant: 'He was oppressed and he was afflicted yet he opened not his mouth.' That verse is followed in Isaiah by a reference to the servant as the 'lamb brought to the slaughter'. Again, the description of Jesus as the paschal lamb is probably due to the influence of this metaphor in Isaiah.

One verse from the suffering servant songs is specifically quoted in Luke 22.37: 'He was reckoned with the transgressors' and is said by Luke to be fulfilled in Jesus' meeting a criminal's death alongside criminals. Luke in fact refers to the suffering servant elsewhere in this gospel showing that this Old Testament figure was very much in mind in formulating his thinking (Luke 1.76; 2.30–32; 3.4–6; 9.35).

The Psalter also seems to have been influential in shaping the passion story. This is particularly true of Psalms 22 and 69. Psalm 22 begins 'My God, my God, why have you forsaken me' which are Jesus' only words from the cross in Matthew and Mark, but the whole of that Psalm seems to have been in the authors' minds. It is in Psalm 22 where we read (in verses 7–8) that 'all who see me laugh me to scorn: they part their lips and wag their heads saying "He trusted in the Lord to deliver him: let him deliver him seeing he delighted in him" '. This quotation probably explains why Mark 15.29 has the ubiquitous Jews, this time at the foot of the cross, not only mock Jesus but also wag their heads and speak words apparently modelled on Psalm 22.8. Psalm 109.25 may also be in mind here: 'I became a reproach to them when they looked on me, they wagged their heads', followed by a cry to God for help in verse 26.

Psalm 22.18 has also influenced a detail in the crucifixion account. This verse states:

> They part my garments among them
> And cast lots for my tunic,

and is quoted in the Fourth Gospel (John 19.23). If we compare John's account of this event with the parallels in Mark 15.24 and Luke 23.34, we can see how the quotation has influenced the telling. In order to have both elements in the quotation fulfilled to the letter, John has to include two items of clothing for Jesus to wear, one that is torn in four, the other which is gambled for. This quotation no doubt lay behind Mark and Luke, but once the verse from the Psalm was set out in full both details in the quotation had to be fulfilled. This is instructive for our understanding of how the early church used the Old Testament.

An example comparable to this may be seen at the beginning of the passion narratives in the story of the triumphal entry. Matthew here (21.5) quotes from Zechariah 9.9:

> Behold your king comes to you meek and sitting on an ass
> And on a colt, the foal of an ass

and interprets it literally as referring to two animals. Thus in his retelling of Mark's narrative (which does not include the quotation) he doubles the number of animals and we are told of an ass *and* a colt. He then paints an incongruous picture of Jesus entering Jerusalem astride both beasts. Strangely, conventions of Hebrew poetry whereby consecutive lines run in parallel, the second line duplicating the thought of the first in synonymous language, are not accepted by those determined at all costs to make an event fit the prophecy.

Psalm 69 like the suffering servant songs of Deutero-Isaiah tells of a righteous sufferer. It is therefore not surprising to find that this Psalm was read with some care and used by the evangelists to explain Jesus' suffering, especially in stories associated with the passion. Verse 9 'for the zeal of your house has eaten me up' is applied by John 2.17 to the cleansing of the temple. The Fourth Gospel takes this episode of the overthrowing of the moneychangers' tables away from the actual passion narrative in order to place it at the beginning of the ministry for the symbolic purpose of showing Jesus as the cleanser of Judaism throughout his career. Zeal for his father's house, that is the temple, is characteristic of John's view of Jesus. It is because of this zeal that Jesus dies, and the 'eating up' of the prophecy is applied to Jesus' death.

Psalm 69.26 speaks of the righteous sufferer being alone and without comforters. This has probably influenced Matthew's and Mark's portrayal of the crucifixion especially as Matthew uses the following verse: 'They gave me gall for my meat and in my thirst they gave me vinegar to drink' at 27.34, where Jesus is offered gall and vinegar. Jesus is also given vinegar to drink at Matthew 27.48 again in fulfilment of this verse in the Psalm. In the Fourth Gospel, Jesus, as so often in this gospel's portrayal of the passion, takes the initiative and states 'I thirst' and is then offered the vinegar (John 19.28–29). Here in John we are specifically told that yet another scriptural prophecy has been fulfilled by this episode.

Among other Psalms quoted in this narrative is Psalm 31.5 'Into your hands I commit my spirit'. This is put on Jesus' lips as his last words in Luke 23.46 and provides a characteristically optimistic Lukan sentiment in contrast to the cry of dereliction which is Jesus' final statement in Mark's, and Matthew's, account of the crucifixion.

Jesus as the paschal lamb has already been referred to in connexion with the suffering servant songs. Such an image of Jesus was of significance elsewhere in the passion narrative especially in the Fourth Gospel, whose chronology allows Jesus to die at the precise moment when the paschal lambs were being slaughtered in preparation for the forthcoming Passover. Paschal elements are particularly prominent in John's telling of the crucifixion as one way of linking Jesus' death with the atoning sacrifice of the lambs in the Exodus narrative. For instance the vinegar offered to Jesus on the cross in John is not put on a lance as it is in Matthew and Mark, but on hyssop, a herb which was an essential ingredient in the Passover meal. In addition one Old Testament passage in particular, which refers to the paschal lamb, is specifically quoted in this gospel with reference to the death of Jesus. At John 19.36, Psalm 34.20 is quoted: 'A bone of him shall not be broken'. Like the paschal lambs Jesus must die unblemished in accord with the Law in Numbers 9.12 and Exodus 12.46. Thus John includes the detail that Pilate's order that Jesus' legs are to be broken so that his death would be expedited is unnecessary. The soldiers sent to carry out the order find Jesus already dead.

The spear thrust into Jesus' side which creates the issue of blood and water is also said by John to be the fulfilment of the prophecy: 'They shall look on him whom they pierced.' This quotation from Zechariah 12.10 appears in the context of the soldiers' proving that Jesus really is dead and their consequent abandonment of Pilate's order. The detail does however fulfil another function, which is symbolic. The issuing of blood and water from a corpse may be medically improbable but, for a gospel imbued with sacramental language and ideas, the need to connect the eucharistic blood and the baptismal water with the death of Jesus finds its place in the crucifixion as a result of the quotation.

Among other quotations in the holy week narratives, the cry of the crowd at the entry of Jesus into Jerusalem 'Hosanna! Blessed is he who comes in the name of the Lord', which is basically the same in all four gospels is from Psalm 118.26. During the Sanhedrin trial at Mark 14.62 Jesus is made to answer the high priest by quoting Daniel 7.13: 'You will see the Son of Man seated at the right hand of power and coming with the clouds of heaven.' Some Old Testament passages are not explicitly quoted but are echoed in the passion story. The false witnesses who are so prominent in both the Sanhedrin and Roman trials and who provide another example of the parallelism between the two trials recall Psalm 27.12: 'For false witnesses have risen up against me and they breathe out cruelty.' The desertion of the disciples is another episode which needed to be justified and explained and again Zechariah was found helpful in this regard. Zechariah 13.7: 'Smite the shepherd and the sheep shall be scattered' is quoted by Mark as an explanation for the inconstancy of the twelve. By contrast the Fourth Gospel implies that the scattering of the disciples was planned and intended by Jesus (John 18.8–9). Both explanations serve as excuses for the behaviour of the disciples.

The prophet Zechariah might also have encouraged the New Testament authors to state that Jesus entered Jerusalem for the last time from the Mount of Olives. To the early Christians steeped in the Old Testament, and in particular the Psalms, Isaiah, and Zechariah, Zechariah 14.4–6 would have been suggestive. Here it is stated that not only on the last day the Lord would go forth from the Mount of Olives and enter Jerusalem, but that that day would be dark. The eclipse of the sun is a detail in the synoptic account of the crucifixion and suggests that this passage from Zechariah was in the evangelists' minds there too.

As with many of these quotations however it is difficult to be specific at each point about the extent to which the prophecy created the event or the extent to which a well-known detail in the tradition about Jesus needed scriptural justification. Both tendencies were at work.

IV

The need to explain the death of Jesus by recourse to the Old Testament is matched to a lesser extent by the need to explain the role of Judas. In the story, Judas was obviously of supreme significance for the early church. That he played some part in the arrest of Jesus is likely to be historic. The tradition that one of Jesus' closest disciples betrayed him is firmly fixed. However much the pro-Pauline branch of the church made the earliest representatives of the pro-Jewish branch of the church based in Jerusalem, such as Peter, appear as ignorant, disbelieving and unaware of Jesus' real message and person during his ministry, it is improbable that they would have invented the treachery of Judas to serve that end had there not been a tradition in existence to this effect. On the contrary, the gospel writers had to explain how and why it was Judas did what he did. Psalm 41.9 speaks of a trusting friend who 'ate of my bread and lifted up his heel against me'. This passage may possibly explain why the gospels have Jesus predict at the last supper that one of those who was dipping his bread into the common dish was to betray him. This passage is however not quoted in the gospels nor does it explain Judas' motive. Luke characteristically, states that the devil entered Judas and caused him to act as he did. Mark has Jesus issue a curse on Judas (14.21) stating it would have been better had Judas not been born. The gospels of Matthew and John attribute Judas' treachery to financial bribery on the part of the Jews. This motive, which fits well with the theme of Jewish wickedness is created according to Matthew 27.9 out of a quotation allegedly from Jeremiah but in fact closer to Zechariah 11.12–13 concerning the pieces of silver. A suitably moralizing end for Judas is also written into this gospel out of this freely adapted prophecy from Jeremiah and Zechariah insofar as the thirty pieces of silver buy a field known as the field of blood. This name gave Matthew the cue to add the detail that Judas hanged himself and was as a consequence buried in the potter's field bought with his blood money.

A different, but again suitably moralistic, end for the villain of the piece appears in Acts 1 where Judas meets a gory death. His burial in the field of blood recalls Matthew, but the death itself is justified with a quotation from the frequently quoted Psalm 69.

The part thus played by the Old Testament is substantial and it seems as if the New Testament writers and the early church combed their Bibles to find texts suitable for explaining not only the death of the Messiah but also the role of Judas.

So far as Judas is concerned we are left with the historical question of what it was he betrayed, and the theological question of his relevance in the career and fate of Jesus. As far as the historical question is concerned, all that Judas seems to have betrayed was Jesus' hiding place in Gethsemane. In the gospels he merely leads the crowds to Jesus and identifies him in the dark. Jesus in fact states in Mark 14.49 that he could have been captured in the temple where he was teaching daily, although, thanks to Mark's telescoping of the chronology, 'daily' here can mean a maximum of only two days. The important point though seems to be that possibly for reasons of civic security Jesus had to be arrested in his hiding-place, and it was this that Judas showed to the crowds. As far as the theological issue is concerned this is not our concern here, but if Jesus was in fact fulfilling divine plans by dying as and when he did, Judas can be but a small cog in a pre-ordained drama enacted in history. As the events were played out on an historical stage Judas, however blameworthy by the standards of the evangelists, was needed if this divine plan was to succeed, which as a divine plan indeed had to succeed in the pre-arranged way.

V

Even if we dismiss the bulk of the trial narratives and passion story as unhistorical and see them as an imaginative construction built from Old Testament proof-texts that does not deny the need for these stories or their essential effectiveness as vehicles for theological teaching.

A rewarding reading of the New Testament gospels is not for historical research at all but is precisely for their theological significance. The purpose in writing of the trials and death of Jesus was primarily to explain the sort of figure the evangelists thought Jesus was. Thus to interpret what the individual authors thought is to be honest to their intentions.

In rewriting the traditions about Jesus the evangelists succeeded in making specific theological statements about Christ in order to convey the significance of the man as they saw him. It is instructive to read the passion narratives in each gospel separately to recognize the distinctive contribution of each writer, and this is especially true of the accounts of Jesus' death. In Mark followed closely by Matthew the picture of Jesus on the cross is essentially tragic. The full horror of the moment of the crucifixion is dwelt on even though here, as in the rest of the New Testament, the ultimate fate of Jesus is known not to have finished at the crucifixion. The earth becomes symbolically darkened at the death of Jesus. To add to the gloom Jesus in these gospels is a man alone, abandoned by his companions, mocked by the onlookers and deserted by God also. The contemporary Jewish conviction was that at point of death man and God were separated: in dying man entered the place of departed spirits, and although there exists in some parts of the Old Testament the hope that eventually God would stretch out his hand and awaken those sleeping in She'ol, in the meantime She'ol was a place where God did not rule. The Epistle to the Hebrews 2.9 like Matthew and Mark shows that Jesus was believed to be 'apart from God' (to follow the most likely text here) at point of death. I Peter in fact states that Jesus was in Hades in the period between his death and resurrection. The early theologians had to account for this period and it is not surprising that I Peter shows how Jesus was gainfully employed in the interval, preaching to the departed spirits. Such an interpretation became normative in Christian doctrine, and in credal formulations, and is in line with Mark's and Matthew's picture of the dying Jesus.

The detail in the synoptic gospels of the veil of the temple being torn in two is, like the preaching in Hades, not to be seen as an historic event but as a theological statement. Here the teaching is that because of Jesus' death the Holy of Holies in the temple was now no longer exclusive: Jesus' death had spelt doom to the existing Jewish rituals. The gospel writers were representatives of the gentile missionary movement in the church when Christian universalism was being increasingly promulgated. One way to preach this was to do as Paul does and show that the age-old promises to Abraham had now passed over to the gentiles and that those living only under the Jewish law were eclipsed. Another way was to say, as the evangelists do, that the veil of the temple was no longer there, and the divine message was open to all.

An extra detail in Matthew's crucifixion account similarly connects a piece of Christian teaching to the death (and subsequent resurrection) of Jesus. This is the passage in Matthew 27.52–53 which says that when Jesus died the faithful dead left their tombs. The theological point is similar to Paul's teaching that as a result of

Christ's death and resurrection those who are believers will share a fate like his. Paul used rhetoric and philosophical writing to make this point – the evangelists, as with the detail about the veil, dramatized their teaching.

In contrast to Matthew's and Mark's gospels, John's Jesus at his death is one whose crucifixion is a moment of glory. The 'lifting up of Jesus from the earth' spoken of by Jesus in John 12.32 is made to refer not just to the resurrection but to the actual crucifixion. Jesus goes confidently to his death in this gospel, willing to drink the cup (John 18.11 compared with Luke 22.42 and synoptic parallels), carrying his own cross, and dying as a paschal lamb with a confident cry of fulfilment on his lips.

In Luke's passion story too Jesus is very much in command of the situation. Luke characteristically continues his theme of forgiveness into the passion. Jesus on the cross forgives those who crucify him and he also forgives one of his fellow prisoners crucified alongside him.

Despite the tragedy of his death particularly stressed in the earlier gospels' account of the agony in Gethsemane and the crucifixion, Jesus in all the gospels is consistently shown to be the one who knows what his destiny will be. He is no mere puppet in the events of history. His death is not shown as an accident. Jesus knows what is to become of him throughout his ministry, and predictions of his ultimate fate are placed on his lips at strategic points in the gospels. These predictions occur three times in each of the synoptic gospels and are intended to show that Jesus was constantly aware of his fate even if the disciples did not understand.

The passion narrative itself also shows Jesus aware of events in advance of their happening. He knows who his betrayer will be; he knows that Peter will deny him three times before daybreak; at the anointing in Bethany in Matthew and Mark he knows his body is not to be anointed at burial (as indeed is the case in the synoptics' as opposed to John's account of the burial); before the triumphal entry he knows that the animal is awaiting him; during the preparations for the last supper he knows that if his disciples go into the city they will meet a man carrying a pitcher of water who will escort them to the upper room. As far as these last two examples are concerned Jesus may indeed have made prior arrangements but such a rationalization of these stories is alien to their purpose. For the evangelist these events are supernaturally foreknown to Jesus, and the fact that they happen as predicted is intended as proof of Jesus' divine status.

An historical approach to all these predictions justifiably encourages us to pronounce that the predictions were written into the story by the writer. But the evangelists' intent was to show that Jesus throughout his career and especially in the events of passion week was doing what had to be done. The crucifixion and the events related to it *had* to be endured. The main purpose in each of the four gospels' accounts of the passion was to show how Jesus fulfilled 'that which was written of the Son of Man', and fulfilled it knowingly.

Texts

Matthew 26–27 and parallels (Mark 14–15; Luke 22–23; John 18–19).

Bibliography

S. G. F. Brandon, *The Trial of Jesus of Nazareth*, Batsford 1969 (Batsford 'Historic Trial' Series I); J. K. Elliott, 'The Anointing of Jesus', *Expository Times* 85, 1974, pp. 105–7; J. K. Elliott, 'When Jesus was Apart from God', *Expository Times*, 83, 1972, pp. 339–41; M. Hengel, *Crucifixion*, SCM Press 1977; E. Lohse, *The History of the Death and Suffering of Jesus Christ*, Fortress Press 1967; P. Winter, *On the Trial of Jesus*, de Gruyter 1961.

5 The First Easter

An investigation into the career of Jesus of Nazareth cannot be based only on his birth, baptism, ministry, trial and death. This sequence needs to be extended to take into account the claim that after his burial he left the tomb and was seen alive by various witnesses. These resurrection appearances are referred to in each of the four New Testament gospels, and the Easter stories are all told as if they were historical events on the same basis as, say, the crucifixion.

Each gospel dates Jesus' resurrection from the Sunday after his burial on Good Friday. We may suspect that originally, when it was announced that Jesus had been raised 'after three days', all that was meant was 'after a short interval', but that, as the tradition developed, this loose expression was made into a literal three-day period; the Friday of the burial, the Saturday in the tomb, and the discovery of the empty tomb some time between darkness after the Saturday and the dawn on Sunday.

The transition between the imprecise and the precise dating of Easter may be seen in the gospels. The earliest gospel, Mark, speaks in its passion predictions of Jesus' being raised 'after three days', whereas the parallels to these predictions in the later gospels alter this to 'on the third day' (cf. Mark 10.34 with Luke 18.33). One reason why the resurrection was dated in this way is that the early Christians in their constant search for Old Testament prophecies that seemed to explain and predict events in Jesus' life came across Hosea 6.2 'After two days he will revive us: on the third day he will raise us up' and made this quotation influence the Easter narrative. Another Old Testament passage, explicitly quoted in Matthew's gospel (12.40), is Jonah 1.17–2.1, which seems to require Jesus to be buried for three days on the analogy of Jonah's 'burial' in the whale for that period.

Whatever the reason for this change from Mark to the later accounts, it is a matter of historic fact that the Christian church owes its foundation to the belief that Jesus Christ of Nazareth was raised from the dead on the third day after his death and burial.

Without this belief the sect of the Nazarenes would have generally died out just as the other messianic groups had disappeared. What nourished the original followers of Jesus and turned them from being frightened men at the time of their master's crucifixion into church founders and missionaries was their belief in the resurrection of Jesus.

The reality of this belief is undeniable by anyone who has read the New Testament or the history of Christianity. But whereas we can assert with conviction that the resurrection belief founded the church, we cannot readily assert as fact the resurrection itself.

The New Testament is the foundation document of the Christian faith and is full of the theological implications of the resurrection. Paul in his letters constantly reminds his readers that the church is living in the new age of the spirit because of Christ's resurrection from the dead. He preaches of a changed relationship between man and God on which man's age old desire for eternal salvation is now pinned. The gospels all tell of the deeds and sayings of Jesus not because these in themselves were necessarily unique, but because they are attributed to the man who was to be raised from the dead; and each gospel ends with the message of Jesus' resurrection. Yet the strange thing is that nowhere does the New Testament attempt to discuss the nature of the resurrection, and nowhere is the happening itself described. At the beginning of the Acts of the Apostles the author feels no awkwardness in describing in a literal way the ascension of Jesus from earth to heaven. Similarly, the gospels find suitable vocabulary with which to depict another supernatural event, namely the alleged transfiguration of Jesus when he speaks with Moses and Elijah. It is therefore strange that no New Testament author attempts to portray the moment when Jesus leaves his tomb, even though stories of raisings from the dead are found in the New Testament gospels and in Acts, the revivification of Lazarus in the Fourth Gospel being the most famous.

Later tradition was slow to describe this episode. The history of Christian art in the West does not show us many examples of the moment of resurrection. We may contrast this with the number of representations of the nativity or the crucifixion.

Although the resurrection itself is not described in the gospels, the stories of the first Easter tell of the visit of women to Jesus' grave, the finding of the empty tomb and the appearances of the risen Jesus. The stories of the walk to Emmaus and of doubting Thomas are well known. Familiarity, though, can often dull the critical faculty. When we analyse the Easter stories critically in the sequence Mark, Matthew, Luke, John, we find inconsistencies between the accounts that make it difficult for us to accept the historicity of any one account in preference to another. This is in contrast to the stories of the passion, which are, by and large, in close parallel in all four gospels.

Mark's Easter story is told in chapter 16.1–8. In this passage we have the visit of the women to the tomb and the angelic messenger's proclamation that Jesus has been raised from the dead. Apart from the surprise ending to this gospel at verse 8, a point where we might well expect to find a story in which Peter and the other disciples meet the risen Jesus in the Galilee, there are a number of other difficulties in the chapter. The motive of the women in visiting the tomb to anoint the body is unlikely, especially in the East where, if a body was to be anointed at all, it would not be done three days after death. Likewise the Jewish repugnance for tombs and ritual abhorrence for things associated with death makes the women's motive even more unlikely. Their fears about being able to enter the sealed tomb at the beginning of the story only add further weight to our arguments. In the event, of course, the resurrection itself makes their plans unnecessary; but the motive attributed to the women in Mark is even more strange when we remember that only two chapters previously Mark has told the story of the anointing of Jesus at Bethany. Whatever the original context and intention of this anointing (and it is likely to be a reminiscence of a coronation rite in which Jesus becomes the anointed one, that is a Messiah), Mark has Jesus in the story interpret the act as an anticipatory anointing of his body for burial, thus rendering any further anointing superfluous. Both this reinterpretation by Mark of the anointing story and the way in which he introduces the Easter story probably reflect the embarrassment of the writer and the early church that at point of death Jesus' body was not accorded the proper burial rites. The perfunctory nature of the burial, as described in the first three gospels, is probably historic: the early church would not have invented this story, although Mark's burial story may only have been included to anticipate the forthcoming discovery of the empty tomb. The burial needs to be described to establish that Jesus really was dead, and that he was buried in an identifiable tomb, if its subsequent emptying is in any sense to be a proof of the resurrection. The women who visit the tomb on the Sunday also need to be described as eye-witnesses of this burial to counter the objection that they visited the wrong tomb.

Matthew avoids these difficulties by having the women visit the tomb merely as sightseers; and John avoids the embarrassment no doubt felt by Mark that Jesus' body needed anointing at such a late date by stating, in contradiction to the synoptics, that Jesus' body *was* anointed by Joseph and Nicodemus at point of death. John, embarrassed by the absence of disciples at the burial (again a detail likely to be historic), makes Joseph of Arimathea 'a disciple' by way of compensation. This enhancement of Joseph of course, continued long after the Fourth Gospel, in the Glastonbury legends. The only reason why Mark has the women visit the tomb is really so that they can be shown it is empty. The empty tomb in Mark's story is, in effect, intended to be proof that Jesus is risen. 'See the place where they laid him', says Mark's angel to underline the statement that Jesus has been raised from the dead. But the empty tomb tradition, to which we shall return later, is a denial of the miraculous element in the resurrection. If the empty tomb proves that Jesus was raised from the dead, then faith in the event itself is of less significance. What Mark tries to do is to depict the finding of the empty tomb as an historic event. But for various reasons, to be discussed below, the episode is unlikely to be historic.

When we return to Matthew's gospel, we can see how the tradition behind Mark's account has been altered and dramatized. For instance, Matthew describes the tomb actually opening before the very eyes of the women (the number of whom he reduces from three to two) unlike Mark and John who say it is already open when the visitors arrive. Matthew's purpose in making this alteration is doubtless to prove that the body could not have been stolen. The opening of the tomb is also intended by Matthew to allow the women to see inside – not to allow Jesus to leave. One is left, however, with the deduction that the body was spirited out of the tomb through solid rock. But of even greater significance, especially for the subsequent development of the Easter stories in the gospel tradition, is the introduction of the risen Jesus into the story. In the rudimentary stage in the development represented here in Matthew 28.9–10 Jesus merely repeats the message given by the angel earlier. Later in the tradition the risen Jesus is given more and more to do and say, so much so that, especially in Luke's and John's Easter accounts, the risen Jesus seems to be little changed from Jesus of Nazareth of the ministry period. In Matthew, the presence of Jesus has made the interpreting angel redundant, and by the time the story reaches John, the angels (John doubles the number) are merely guards at the tomb.

Having thus opened the way for such elaboration of the tradition and for the creation of other stories, Matthew then completes what was implicit in Mark by including a story in which Jesus is seen by the eleven disciples. Jesus here at the end of Matthew's gospel is a rather stylized figure unlike the later portrayals in Luke's and John's Easter accounts; but we do now have a story in which Jesus is seen by his disciples in the Galilee as promised. Jesus' encounters with the disciples are the most common type of post-resurrection appearance in the New Testament; and it is significant that no neutral witnesses see the risen Jesus. In that final story (Matt. 28.16–20), which forms the climax and conclusion to Matthew's gospel, the words attributed to Jesus summarize the whole book. In fact, all words attributed to Jesus in the resurrection stories are likely to come not from Jesus but from the evangelist. Matthew's risen Jesus speaks like Matthew, whereas in the Fourth Gospel Jesus speaks like John the theologian.

When we turn to Luke's gospel, there are certain similarities between his Easter morning narrative and the other gospels' accounts; for example, Luke follows Mark in the motive attributed to the women's visit to the tomb; and he resembles John in having two angels; but there are differences. The number of women is greatly increased, and the statement in Luke 24.22f. contradicts Matthew and John by denying that any women had seen Jesus at the tomb.

The greatest difference in Luke, though, is that several resurrection appearances are described, and all take place in and around Jerusalem, not the Galilee. For Luke and Acts the centre of the Jewish world, Jerusalem, is the hub from which Christianity spread out to the gentile world. For Matthew and Mark the geography of Palestine has a different significance and symbolism. For them Jerusalem is the place where Jesus is killed, and the Galilee, the area where revelations take place, is identified as 'Galilee of the Gentiles' (Matt. 4.15–16) leading to the world-wide mission. Luke rounds off the Easter stories more successfully than the other evangelists with the ascension story, which is a device for terminating these post-resurrection appearances.

The increased number of stories, together with the greater attempts at realism in Luke's gospel, is continued in the Fourth Gospel, which similarly has several (but different) Easter narratives. Except in the appendix to this gospel (John 21), John follows Luke in having the appearances set in Jerusalem. Another feature of the Easter stories in this gospel is that great stress is placed on the identification of the risen Christ as Jesus of Nazareth.

This sketch of the inconsistencies and changes in the story began with Mark. But really an historical investigation into the events of the first Easter should go back further still and get behind Mark's story. The earliest written account of the post-resurrection appearances in the New Testament is of course Paul's. As the only New Testament author who claims to have seen the risen Lord, Paul's testimony is obviously of supreme importance. Paul in I Corinthians 15 states that the resurrection took place 'according to the scriptures', that is in the Old Testament. But Paul could not quote chapter and verse. A crucified or suffering Messiah was not expected in the Old Testament; hence a resurrected Messiah was not predicted either. Paul's statement must mean that in some way Jesus was the fulfilment of Old Testament prophecy, and that, if he as Messiah was raised from the dead, then somehow and somewhere in the Old Testament such a prediction should be capable of being located. We have often seen in the New Testament how the early Christians did seem to search their scriptures diligently to make Old Testament prophecies fit Jesus. But the resurrection seems to have baffled them, and no adequate Old Testament quotation is ever produced. Cleopas and his companion on their walk to Emmaus are told merely that biblical witnesses anticipate the resurrection.

In I Corinthians 15 Paul lists several people who are said to have seen Jesus after his death. This list includes an appearance to Paul himself. If the accounts of the Damascus road experience in Acts, when Paul sees a blinding light and hears the voice of Jesus, are descriptions of that appearance to Paul referred to in I Corinthians, then what is being referred to as a 'resurrection appearance' by Paul is obviously of a different genre from the resurrection appearances dramatized in the gospels. If Paul assumed his experience of the risen Jesus was in any sense comparable to the visions granted to the original disciples in his list (as doubtless he would), then what he thought they had experienced was radically different from what the evangelists later described. Also, unlike the gospels, Paul does no more than provide a list. There are no details of how, where or when the Easter encounters took place or what happened. Similarly in Paul there is a complete silence about the empty tomb; and it is likely that Paul did not know of this tradition. In any case, he is more interested in the present reality and future significance of the resurrection than in the purely historical aspect of the event.

The material in the early chapters of the Acts of the Apostles also contains elements that, we can presume, predate the gospel material; and in these early chapters the resurrection proclamation is remarkably similar to the primitive teaching in Paul's letters. Again, there is no mention of Jesus' empty tomb, even though Acts 2.29 shows knowledge of the existence of David's grave. In Acts, as in Paul's letters, we find only the proclamation that Jesus, who had been killed and buried, was raised from the dead. And this is the point where Mark takes up the story by developing that proclamation and using it as a vehicle for conveying much theological teaching. There is thus a development through the gospel tradition from the basic report that Jesus is risen to fully dramatized accounts in which Jesus is seen, speaks and acts.

From this analysis of the stories of the first Easter in the gospels it is obvious that we cannot reconcile the accounts or make a harmony of them. The foundations on which the theological teaching on resurrection is based are different in each gospel, which shows that the early church's belief in Jesus' resurrection did not depend on uniform teaching. The stories, however, can be summarized. The elements in common between the accounts of the first Easter morning are that, after Joseph has placed Jesus' body in a rock tomb and sealed it with a stone, one, two, three, or several women find that stone rolled away on the third day. They enter the tomb and see a young man, or two men, or an angel sitting (according to Mark and Matthew) or standing (according to Luke) in the tomb. The women are then shown the place where Jesus was laid and told he has been raised. They are then given a message to pass on to the disciples. In Luke and Matthew they do so; but in Mark they disobey this command as they are struck dumb – a symptom frequently found in biblical narratives when a person is said to be privy to a divine proclamation. So far as the remaining post-resurrection stories are concerned, there is little common ground between the details in the gospels. The frequency and nature of the appearances and the participants and circumstances are all different. We cannot treat any of the Easter stories as historical; but we cannot doubt the paramount significance of the narratives for the evangelists; and it is of great profit to examine the motives of the authors who included them. There is no independent witness to the Easter events outside the New Testament; so one must make use of the gospel material alone.

If the gospels are to be seen as missionary documents, then the main purpose of the stories in them is to evoke faith. The Fourth Gospel states such an aim at the end of the first draft of the gospel (John 20.30–31: 'Jesus did many other signs in the presence of his disciples which are not written in this book, but these are written that you may believe that Jesus is the Christ, the Son of God, and that believing you may have life through his name'). Before this faith could be kindled, however, doubts had to be dismissed. In fact, one of the main motifs running through the stories of Jesus' reappearances is that of doubt. As we have already stated, the resurrection of Jesus was not expected; and therefore both the disciples and subsequent generations of believers had first to be convinced of its reality. What the gospel writers attempt to do for their contemporaries is to show that the first believers, too, had doubts, but that these were resolved. Doubting Thomas is the most famous of those who needed convincing. The patently apologetic purpose of this episode is underlined by John's postscript, where he says (20.29b) 'Blessed are those who have not seen yet have believed', which included the vast bulk of John's contemporaries. The resurrection stories, in other words, are intended to be proofs that Jesus really was raised from the dead. Doubts about this among the evangelists' contemporaries were read back into the life of the immediate post-Easter church. The disciples in Luke think that talk of resurrection is nonsense; the walkers on the way to Emmaus are convinced of Jesus' presence only when he reveals himself to them in breaking the bread (presumably a characteristic and recognizable gesture); Mary in the garden thinks Jesus is the gardener. The evangelists knew that such proofs provided by Jesus' reappearances on earth were not available at the time of writing; hence the reappearance stories are described as occurring rather improbably in a limited period. Luke, for instance, ends the resurrection stories with the story of Jesus' ascension, although he does not indicate the duration between Easter and ascension. It is left for the second volume in the two-part work, Luke–Acts, to specify that this interval was forty days, a number of symbolic significance in Jewish writing. The Fourth Gospel, too, in Jesus' command to Mary to cease holding him as he is about to ascend to the Father similarly provides a *terminus ad quem* for the reappearances. Paul's list of resurrection appearances suggests that he, too, is aware that the appearance granted to him was not within the restricted period in which the appearances to the original disciples took place. Despite the necessary limiting of the Easter events, the purpose of these stories is clearly to provide ostensibly historic proofs of the resurrection to putative believers, so that their doubts should disappear just as those of the first disciples are said to have been removed.

Another motif, particularly in the developed tradition, is the attempt to stress the corporeality of Jesus' risen body. In Matthew and the Fourth Gospel we read that Jesus' body was capable of being touched: in the Fourth Gospel the wounds of his recent crucifixion are visible: in Luke, Jesus eats broiled fish. There is thus a continuity between the risen Lord and Jesus of Nazareth; even Mark makes this point – his angel in 16.7 refers us back to the pre-crucifixion period with the words 'as he told you'. Such reminders of Jesus' ministry are obviously intentional. And yet at the same time there is an attempt to show that there is a difference between the two Jesuses. For instance, in some of the Easter stories Jesus passes through closed doors; he reappears and disappears at will; and he is not readily recognizable as he was during the period of his ministry.

The New Testament gospels' Easter stories appear to reflect here two different traditions – one spiritual, one physical. The nature of Jesus' resurrected body was understandably one that troubled the earliest believers; and is a trouble reflected not only in the Easter narratives in the gospels but also in the earlier story where Jesus and the Sadducees are depicted as discussing the nature of the afterlife, and also in I Corinthians 15, where Paul attempts to describe the idea of bodily resurrection – an essentially Jewish belief – to an audience obviously reared on Hellenistic philosophical ideas about the immortality of the soul. In the Jewish environment in which Christianity began, whenever Jesus' afterlife was being spoken of, resurrection was the natural way to describe it. Coupled with this, there may well have been an attempt in the early church to counter embryonic docetic or gnostic heresies about Jesus' body by emphasizing that after death Jesus was still body. These heresies taught that matter was essentially evil, and that it was inconceivable for the son of God to appear in a human body – either before or after death. The evangelists, on the other hand, were at pains to stress that Jesus was the 'word become *flesh*' during his ministry, and that even after his death he was no mere spirit. Luke actually has the risen Jesus say he is not a spirit but has flesh and bones. The Christians' attempt in the New Testament to preserve this essentially Jewish concept of describing life after death is the reason why so many of the Easter narratives in the gospels contain contradictions and difficulties. There is a dichotomy between a spiritualized concept of afterlife, which many of the details in the stories presuppose, and a fully physical corporeal body demanded by the tradition's background and by the evangelists' theology. One can only resolve such difficulties by isolating the separate elements and by explaining these along theological, not historical, lines.

A further *theological* point made by the Easter narratives is that Jesus in his resurrected state is visible only to those who have faith. He is seen only by those who followed him in his lifetime or who subsequently were believers. The story in Matthew of the first Easter Sunday is significant. In this story Jesus is not seen by those guarding the tomb. The guards are not permitted to see the risen Lord and consequently have to 'fall asleep' just at the crucial moment when he appears. Neutral bystanders are not privy to Christophanies. The appearance is intended only for the women; and the purpose of the story is to show how their faith was evoked by an 'historic' event.

The Easter narratives try to give positive proofs of the reality of Jesus' resurrection to counter objections to resurrection belief that the early Christians met in their evangelizing. Of supreme and obvious importance is the need to say that Jesus really died. The burial story in the gospels is intended to be that proof, and is unlikely to have been told for its own sake. In the developed tradition in John's gospel, Pilate is made to ascertain clearly the fact of Jesus' death. This detail is present because some were arguing that Jesus did not die, and that consequently resurrection can be explained away by saying that after the deposition Jesus awoke and left his tomb.

The empty tomb is intended to be further proof that Jesus is raised, albeit in this case negative proof. A literal Hebraic view of resurrection as the resuscitation of corpses is found in Matthew 27.52–53, which is a theological insertion into the crucifixion account. For Matthew, belief in the resurrection is necessarily dependent on one leaving one's tomb. If the earliest belief was that Jesus had been raised from the dead, then logically, at least to Matthew and the Jewish mind, he could no longer be in the tomb.

But this negative proof of resurrection seems to have caused as many problems as it solved. It obviously left the way open for objectors to claim that, if the tomb was empty, then the body was stolen. This is a claim that Matthew and John in their different ways attempt to disprove. In John, Mary assumes that the disappearance of Jesus' corpse is due to the disciples' having removed it. She is soon to be discouraged from holding this view by being shown the burial clothes and head-bindings still in place in the tomb, the inference being that, if his body had been stolen, then these would have gone too. We must also infer from this story that John here thought of resurrection in a spiritual way, and that Jesus was spirited out of his bindings and out of the closed tomb. In Matthew's gospel, on the other hand, the rumour that Jesus' body was stolen is attributed to the wickedness of the Jews. The story tells how the guards, whose purpose in guarding the tomb is thwarted by the resurrection, are asked to put about the rumour that the disciples had stolen the corpse. Many of Matthew's contemporaries were probably hearing this allegation from those opposed to the Christian proclamation; hence he had to explain how such a rumour arose. We may legitimately say that the stories of the theft of Jesus' body *were* rumours put about by opponents of the Christian message, and that these followed rather than preceded the stories of the empty tomb. It is unlikely that the gospels tried to cover up an actual theft.

The earliest disciples of Jesus did not expect his death or his resurrection. The despair of the disciples at the crucifixion is likely to be historical. It is less probably an invention of the early church: as time went by, the early church tended to accord to those who had known the earthly Jesus a place of respect and honour; and it was an embarrassment to record an episode in which the disciples of Jesus are depicted as deserting their master at his arrest. The desertion is poignantly described in the dramatic and effective legend of Peter's threefold denial of allegiance to Jesus before the maid of the high priest, which parallels the trial his master is undergoing before the high-priest himself. It is unlikely that the disciples would have deserted Jesus if he had prepared them for his resurrection. Either he did not speak of resurrection to them, or else they did not understand him when he did. The former is more probable. The gospels do include predictions on Jesus' lips that he is to rise again after his death; but these are thought by many scholars to be prophecies after the event, put there by the evangelists. It is often said in the gospels at these points that the disciples do not understand his predictions. This is in order to explain the embarrassing desertion later. Certainly it is significant that the resurrection is represented as playing very little part in Jesus' teaching. This is particularly surprising in view of the prominence given to the resurrection in the Acts of the Apostles and in the Pauline epistles.

So far we have seen that the gospels' Easter narratives include what are intended to be positive and negative proofs of the resurrection, together with attempts to describe the nature of the resurrected body itself. These narratives are also useful vehicles for other theological and doctrinal teaching, some of which may be simply listed.

In John 20.23 we notice that John connects the forgiveness of sins with the presence of the risen Christ. This, too, is the purpose of the story in John 21 with its threefold declaration of forgiveness for Peter reversing the threefold denial before the crucifixion. More significantly the resurrection stories are used to indicate that the foundation of the church began with the resurrection. It is the risen Lord at the end of Matthew who sends forth his missionaries. Similarly, at the end of Luke the mission of the church beginning at Jerusalem is initiated by a command of the risen Jesus. In Pauline theology the new life of the Christian church is connected intimately with Jesus. He is the first-fruits of those raised from the dead; but those who are *en Christo* are able to share with him in a resurrection like his. In the meantime, says Paul, the church is living in the age of the spirit directed by the risen Lord, and the Christians are told they are the new creation. John puts this more symbolically in his Easter story when the risen Lord breathes on his disciples. He is giving them the spirit of the new age, just as God in Genesis 2 inaugurated the life of man by 'breathing into his nostrils the breath of life'.

The Easter stories are, therefore, no mere attempts to describe allegedly historical events. Paul, as stated earlier, is more concerned with the present and future significance of resurrection for the Christians to whom he wrote his letters than with the historical details of Christ's own resurrection. Nor can the gospels be used as historical documents for proof of the resurrection. They are theological documents, using the resurrection story to convey theological and apologetic teaching, and in this respect are not so different from Paul's teaching as a first glance might suggest.

Having dismissed the historical reliability of the Easter stories in the gospels, we may legitimately ask if the resurrection itself did happen. An historical approach demands that we reply that the resurrection was not an event in Jesus' career comparable to his birth and death. The resurrection *was* an event, but only in the history of the church. Yet it is difficult to describe how or why belief in Jesus' resurrection began. The traditional Christian explanation would obviously say merely that the belief grew because Jesus did rise, and because the gospels say he was seen after his death. But, as we have indicated, this view has its own difficulties. On the other hand, one hesitates to speak of resurrection experience in terms of subjective visions or hallucinations – certainly the New Testament writers do not describe it in this way; and they could have done so if they had so wished. Something like Peter's vision in Acts, or the dream sequences in the infancy narratives, could have been utilized to describe the resurrection appearances. Resurrection to the first believers was something different, and had to be described in terms appropriate to what they claimed had been a new experience. Thus it is described in a personal style, not as a vision but almost as if Jesus himself was present.

The way in which the belief began, and why it was expressed in the way it was, may be described in the following manner. Resurrection belief arose first among those who had known Jesus in his lifetime. After his death, they had a vivid and personal feeling that Jesus was in some sense still with them and was guiding them. Later generations could not, of course, think of the risen Jesus, as did those who had known him in his ministry; but even they could say, as Paul did, that they had an overwhelming and personal feeling that the spirit of Jesus was influencing them. Jesus was 'risen' because his message, personality, power and influence continued after his death. Jesus' guidance and inspiration outlived him, and for the believer he was still living. Resurrection was the natural first-century Jewish way of describing this continuing influence.

In a milieu in which views on afterlife were expressed in terms of the resurrection of individuals by some circles at least within Judaism, it is perhaps not surprising that the earliest followers of Jesus should have spoken of their master's abiding influence, continuing presence and guidance, as his resurrection. Some people thought that John the Baptist had been raised from the dead (Mark 6.14ff.), and that Elijah's spirit lived on in Elisha (II Kings 2.15) and legends exist in the New Testament telling of people who were raised from the dead by Jesus and, later, by Peter and Paul. All these provide the environment in which belief in Jesus' resurrection took shape and flourished. These Jewish ideas would and did find favour in the Hellenistic world outside, where stories of dying and rising gods were part of the native folk myths. Thus to talk of the resurrection of Jesus would not have seemed so strange.

We suspect that the earliest impression of Jesus' abiding power was felt after his death during the communal meals for which the followers of Jesus seem to have continued to meet. It is significant how many of the Easter narratives have a eucharistic setting. John 21 speaks of Jesus' eating with his disciples; Cleopas and his friend recognize Jesus only in the breaking of bread; the revelations to the ten in the upper room in John's gospel, and to the ten plus Thomas a week later, seem to have a setting similar to that of the Last Supper. When they met for such meals after his death it is probable that Jesus' erstwhile colleagues reminisced about his career, and felt that in some way the memory of him was so strong that they could and did say 'he is alive'. Those who had known him would obviously still think of him in a corporeal way. Later generations would obviously have no such memory to work on, and would tend to have only a spiritualized image of Christ. Perhaps this is why we have the two images in the New Testament – the physical resurrected body belonging to the earliest tradition and the spiritualized risen Lord, emanating from those predominantly gentile Christians who had not seen Jesus before his death.

The early believers were quick to grasp the significance of resurrection, and proclaimed a changed relationship with God. The sin of Adam, which had resulted in death, had now been reversed, and Christ was hailed as the new Adam, bringing not death into the world but life. The age-old cycle of cause and effect, that is sin and death, which started at the fall had now been broken. Those incorporated mystically into union with Christ through baptism were now seen to have the certain hope of an eternal life like his. His death and resurrection at one point in time were said to have enduring effect for all mankind. Christians were seen to be living in the new age of the spirit, and were a 'new creation', as a result of Jesus' breaking the power of death. Morality and ethics could be put on a new footing – no longer were these the *sine qua non* of being saved. Instead, having been declared to be justified by grace, moral behaviour is seen by Paul and others as the logical pattern of Christian life. One no longer sinned in a body that could die; sin was now seen as an act against a body destined for eternity. Thus Christ's resurrection is seen in the New Testament as a paradigm for the future destiny of his people. He is but the first-fruits of those raised from the dead.

Such is a brief summary of some New Testament teaching of resurrection. In it attention is taken away from the purely historical element in the proclamation. Once Jesus' abiding presence was spoken of in terms of resurrection, with all that this meant about breaking out of death's grasp, then the new and revolutionary New Testament theology gave a universalism and timelessness to Christ's person and message. Resurrection belief, implying a death in which all men share, obviously had a new meaning of such value that Paul could say to the Corinthians that, if the resurrection were not true, and if Christ had not been raised, then his teaching was in vain, and the Corinthians' faith too was in vain, and that of all men Christians were most to be pitied for their false hope. For Paul and the writers of the New Testament the resurrection of Jesus was obviously a reality. Our conclusion, though, is that the resurrection of Jesus was an event only in the minds and lives of Jesus' followers. It cannot be described as an historic event. The Easter story is a faith legend, not an objective eye-witness report; but it is a myth that the Christian church through the centuries has found to be a continuing inspiration.

Texts

Matthew 28; Mark 16; Luke 24; John 20–21.

Bibliography

J. E. Alsup, *The Post-Resurrection Appearance Stories of the Gospel Tradition*, Calwer and SPCK 1975; C. F. Evans, *Resurrection and the New Testament*, SCM Press 1970, reissued 1981; R. H. Fuller, *The Formation of the Resurrection Narratives*, SPCK 1972, reissued 1981; P. Gardner-Smith, *The Narratives of the Resurrection*, Methuen 1926; H. Grass, *Ostergeschehen und Osterberichte*, Vandenhoeck and Ruprecht 1956; W. Marxsen, *The Resurrection of Jesus of Nazareth*, SCM Press 1970; C. F. D. Moule (ed.), *The Significance of the Message of Resurrection for Faith in Jesus Christ*, SCM Press 1968.

6 Christianity's First History Book

The ministry and teaching of Christ resulted in his attracting a small group of followers who perpetuated his memory and message after his death. But the origins of Christianity were humble and inauspicious. The religion began with an itinerant preacher in a remote part of the Roman Empire, and seemed to be doomed to failure when the preacher was crucified in Jerusalem, leaving his disciples disillusioned and leaderless.

Yet far from dying with him, Christ's message not only lived on but spread rapidly. Within thirty years of his death groups of people who believed in him as a new saviour were to be found throughout the mediterranean lands. The rapid and successful spread of this new religion is for the pious Christian a proof and vindication of its inherent truth, and an indication that the earliest propogators of the faith were divinely inspired.

For non-believers the ease with which the religion took hold can be explained by several different factors. Doubtless the *Pax Romana* aided communications between countries. The period in question, AD 30–60 was also one of comparative peace, so that travel and transport were generally unhindered. In addition the language used by the earliest Christians, Hellenistic Greek, was the lingua franca of the mediterranean world, and this made the evangelists readily comprehensible.

The network of synagogues throughout the mediterranean diaspora, with their 'Godfearing' non-Jews on the fringes, provided the Christians with a ready-made focal-point with which to start their conversions. Other factors favourable to the spread of the new 'philosophy' were the apparent disillusionment in many sections of society with the traditional religious practices of Greece and Asia-Minor, and the attraction that the Christian message held – especially for the downtrodden.

None of these factors, though, would have been of any value had there not been a strong and dedicated group of Christians, intent on trying to win others to their cause. Theologians throughout the centuries have tried to explain why Christianity was (and is) attractive, essential, and unavoidable. Doubtless, various aspects of Christian preaching appealed to different people in different ways. The paradoxes in its teaching often proved to be its strength. The enigmatic centre of the religion, its divine yet human saviour, provided both an other-worldly and an identifiable leader; and its idealistic yet commonsense ethical precepts no doubt aided its transmission. But, above all, the sheer adaptability of so much of Christianity made it a religion that could be tailored to suit the background of many groups in the ancient world – Jewish, Greek, pagan, free, slave, male, female, rich, poor.

The speed with which Christianity left its exclusively Jewish origins, and put down roots in the gentile world, was not only a source of surprise and inspiration to the early church, but also a cause of friction. One near-contemporary attempt to record the growth of Christianity, and to iron out the early schisms, was the Acts of the Apostles. This book was written before the end of the first century, and, among other things, purports to be the first history book of the Christian church.

The book of Acts covers the first thirty years or so of the church's life, beginning in Jerusalem shortly after Christ's death and ending in Rome during Paul's imprisonment there (normally dated at about 62–65). It appears to give a detailed description of how Christianity left Jerusalem, the centre of the old Jewish religion, and reached Rome, the capital of the Empire. That Christianity began in Palestine and reached Rome very quickly is not disputable. But the historical value of much else in Acts is.

Historical books in the ancient world cannot be consulted uncritically if one is concerned to abstract from them pure facts. Nor, of course, should they be used in this way: it is alien to their purpose. And this is especially true of religious books, of which the Acts of the Apostles is obviously one. Its author and the author of the third gospel were the same – traditionally assumed to be Luke the physician. Acts is the second of the two volume work Luke – Acts, and, like its predecessor, is written above all to justify the veracity of the new religion. Both are dedicated to a symbolic Theophilus, which means 'lover of God'. This suggests that the readership of the two books was more likely to be interested in theology than in history. The supernatural events and the miracles described in Acts as well as the legendary material to which religious writing is often prone, brands it as a work whose historical content is, to say the least, suspect.

One of the major sources against which we can check much of what is recorded in Acts is the writings of Paul. Several details referred to in his surviving letters do not tally with the description of the same events in Acts. Moreover, the characteristic theology of Paul is conspicuously absent from the speeches of Paul as recorded in Acts. This suggests that, as so often in ancient literature, the attribution of speeches to leading characters is more likely to be a mark of editorial imagination than an attempt to provide verbatim records. Many of the other differences between Paul's letters and Acts are capable of being reconciled by conservatives determined to deflect apparent criticism of scriptural infallibility. But one of the major areas in which Paul's record differs from that of Acts is in the description of the way in which Christianity spread. Paul often recalls the antagonisms and conflicts that marred his easy contact with gentiles. Much of this came from 'Judaizers', that is, from those in the church who were opposed to Paul's converting non-Jews to Christianity without first converting them to Judaism or, at least, making them observe the Jewish law as a prerequisite. Accounts of these conflicts may be seen *inter alia* in Philippians 3, II Corinthians 11, Romans 9, and especially in Galatians 2 and 3. These chapters show that the early Christians were not so amicably united as Acts seems to show. Chapter 8 will discuss this issue in detail.

Acts tells of Christianity's easy transition from being dominated by Jews to being primarily a gentile faith. The Christian message in Acts is described as spreading out in ever-increasing circles. Acts begins with the church in Jerusalem, and this section concludes with a progress report in 6.7. Then we are told of the spread of Christianity into Palestine, culminating in another summary statement in 9.31. From 9.32–12.24 we read of the church's reaching Antioch. and from 12.25–16.5 of its extension into Asia-Minor. From 16.6–19.20 the church reaches Europe, and from there to the end of the book we read of Paul's journey to Rome. The structure of the book thus suggests editorial planning and manipulation.

A close examination of the work shows that the impression given of a steady forward march is false. Paul, the pro-gentile hero of Acts, finds Christians in Rome when he arrives there; and, in fact, he had earlier sent a letter to the Christians in Rome, most of whom were strangers to him. The tradition is that Peter had founded the church in Rome; but Acts says nothing about this important development. This is significant in view of the strategic importance of a Christian community at the centre of the Empire. It did not suit the purpose of Acts to record the foundation of the Roman church by so prominent an advocate of the Jerusalem-based church. It is perhaps as significant to note that Peter is 'written out' of Acts with the enigmatic words in 12.17: '(Peter) left the house and went off *elsewhere*'. So vague a statement is uncharacteristic of our author. One suspects he deliberately suppressed further information about Peter's missionary successes. (Peter is mentioned again in chapter 15, where he is merely the symbolic spokesman at the Council of Jerusalem, of which the chairman is now the new church leader, James.)

It is clear that the purpose of Acts was not to give a day-to-day record of Christian origins, but in a broader survey to prove to its readers how it was God's intention that the Christian message should spread to gentiles. In other words, Acts is propaganda for the pro-gentile branch of the church led by Paul; and it was this branch that ultimately succeeded in preserving Christianity by broadening its appeal. The 'so-called pillars of the church' who are 'reputed to be something', as Paul bitingly refers to the Jerusalem church-leaders in Galatians 2, were the ones who tried to keep Christianity within Judaism, or, rather, to make Judaism Christian. The speech attributed to Stephen in Acts 7, dealing with the destiny of the Jews, is really propaganda against these Judaizers, and provides the theoretical justification for turning to the gentiles. By contrast, the speech attributed to Paul on the Areopagus, at the centre of the Greek philosophical world, is doubtless intended – despite Paul's conspicuous lack of success in Athens – to be a model for preaching to gentiles.

The Judaizers' policy had little appeal or real success. No wonder, then, that the advocates of the policy were jealous of Paul's evangelizing. Acts, however, tries to diminish the differences between the factions, even to the extent of spending much space describing the Council of Jerusalem. At this Council Paul is said to have agreed to a code of conduct whereby gentile converts to Christianity would be obliged to accept some minimal requirements of Jewish law and practice. Paul's own letters show no knowledge of such a Council or of decisions that would have had the effect of bridling his freedom. Nor does early church history suggest that these Jewish precepts were ever observed or demanded of converts. The sole purpose of the account of the Council in Acts 15 is to show that both sides of the church, pro-gentile and pro-Jewish, met on common ground. This is in part due to the fact that Acts was written after the heat of the moment, whereas Paul's letters bear the stamp of immediacy. As a result, Acts tends to be idealistic. The conflicts with the pro-Jewish leaders of Christianity died out with the fall of Jerusalem in 70; and by the time Acts was written twenty more years had elapsed, so that it was no longer relevant or useful to report these old antagonisms.

'The Acts of the Apostles' is perhaps a misleading title to the book (which was originally untitled, like all New Testament books). It leads one to expect a full description of the missionary activity of many, if not all, of those designated apostles. In fact, only Peter and Paul predominate; and for very good reasons. It was the intention of Acts to show the steady and amicable progress of Christianity. It describes the transition from the Jewish Christian community in Jerusalem, led by Peter, to the world-wide church fostered by Paul by concentrating on the activities of these two leading figures. Thus the deliberate blurring of the differences between the two sides in the primitive church is personified in its two leading advocates. The sharp antagonism between the sides, explicit in Paul's own letters and implicit in much of Acts, is blunted by the many references to Paul as a loyal Jew. Like the Jerusalem church leaders Paul is shown to approve of circumcision (16.3), and to take a Nazarite vow (18.18f.); he addresses Jews in Aramaic (22.3) and is pleased to call himself a Pharisee (23.6). Paul is thereby shown to be as Jewish as Peter. Paul (as he himself often pointed out in his letters) belonged to the traditional stock of Christianity. From Peter's side Acts 10 tells a story in which Peter in Caesarea makes an attempt (albeit half-heartedly) to reach a gentile audience, much to his Jerusalem colleagues' disapproval.

Acts, however, is a book that favours the Pauline approach; and as such it is not surprising that Paul is the real hero. It is, as we have seen, he who is credited with reaching Rome with the gospel from Jerusalem. The climax of Acts is Paul's missionary activity in Rome, undiminished and unrestricted even under house-arrest. There is no record of Paul's death, a fact that has caused many scholars to date Acts earlier than 65, the traditional date of his death. But this does not follow. The importance of Acts is to show how Paul reached Rome. Its readers probably knew the rest of the story of Paul and the church. What they needed to be told was how the pro-gentile Christian message reached the centre of the gentile world; and Acts does this, crediting Paul with the success. To have portrayed Paul, the loyal Roman citizen, as a martyr at Roman hands would have been not only inappropriate but embarrassing to a church concerned to win favour among the governing authorities. Paul is consequently portrayed as a model of endurance, and as such is made an example to later Christians, especially in times of persecution. The recording of Paul's death could have defeated this aim.

The dominance of Paul's message and work is evidenced in another way in Acts. Paul is consistently shown to be as successful as Peter, and often *more* successful. Pauline Christianity needed Peter and the Jerusalem church to provide it with roots and establish its continuity with Jesus of Nazareth, whom they *all* preached about; but Peter – as in Mark's gospel – is frequently described as being an unsatisfactory Christian. This attitude contrasts with Matthew's gospel, in many ways the most pro-Jewish of the four gospels, which shows a special interest in Peter's supremacy as we shall see in the next chapter.

Doublets and parallels within Acts suggest that many legends and tales about Peter were later used and adapted by the Paulinist author with reference to Paul. For instance, both Peter and Paul begin their respective ministries by healing a lame man (3.2f. and 14.8f.). (In this they are both being portrayed as imitators of Christ.) Both meet magicians (8.9f. and 13.6f.). Like Jesus, both men are said to raise the dead (9.36f. and 20.9f.). Both men, like their Lord, are popular miracle-workers (5.15f. and 19.11f.). Both escape from gaol through miraculous intervention (12.7f. and 16.26f.). Similarly, much of the teaching attributed to Peter is similar to the content of preaching attributed later to Paul.

Paul is thereby consistently described as a successful representative of the pro-gentile church. There is less interest in him as a person. Certainly one cannot write the biography of Paul from Acts. Many events in his life are known only from his own letters. If the author of Acts knew of these events, he chose not to give them in his own work. Paul in Acts is predominantly an idealized figure, personifying the gentile missionary movement; and details about his life are subordinated to this general aim.

Acts, however, is concerned not only with idealizing Paul but also with making edifying and elevating statements about the church. It tries to present a picture of a unanimous church practising communalism, even though the story in chapter 5, which tells of a man and woman who are divinely struck dead for failing to admit they were not sharing their property, destroys the normally idealistic picture that the author has elsewhere attempted to impose on tradition. So, too, does the story in 6.1f., which shows there was a split in Jerusalem between Greek- and Aramaic-speaking Christians. Another impression the author tries to impose on his traditions is that the church was thriving; but again there are indications (in several of the early chapters) that Christians were clashing with the authorities. In other words, our author has not always been entirely successful in imposing consistently his own view of the church on the traditions and material he had at his disposal.

Yet despite these inconsistencies and the many apologetic and legendary traits in the book, Acts makes fascinating reading. It is no dry or crude polemic. There are vivid and dramatic stories describing encounters between the early preachers and – among others – the Ethiopian eunuch (chapter 8), Governor Felix (chapter 24), and King Agrippa (chapter 25). The descriptions of Saul's conversion, and of Stephen's martyrdom, are memorable and effective vehicles for theological teaching; and the long, detailed and stirring sea yarn, describing Paul's hazardous journey to Rome, is a classic of its type. The humour with which the Pentecost events are narrated makes it a vignette of religious literature.

Much of what is described as having happened is unlikely to have occurred as reported; but the contemporary world, which provides the background of the events, is the real world, in which appeals to Caesar, contacts with synagogues and with various social groups, all have the ring of verisimilitude. The first-century milieu, in which the early Christian communities took root and thrived, is no make-believe scenario. Though Acts is an apologia for pro-gentile Christianity, what strikes the reader is the *narrative* art of the author.

There is little ethical exhortation; and references to Jesus' teaching are almost completely absent. The theological content of the speeches that do occur is repetitive, primitive and often naïve. Acts does not aspire to poetic fantasy or apocalyptic imagery. The author's main interest is in events and personalities; and for this reason alone Acts may justifiably rank as the first history book of Christianity.

Texts

Relevant samples from the Acts of the Apostles could be chapters 4, 9, 17 and 27–28.

Bibliography

F. F. Bruce, *Paul: Apostle of the Free Spirit*, Paternoster 1977; E. J. Epp, *The Theological Tendency of Codex Bezae Cantabrigensis in Acts*, Society for New Testament Study Monograph 3, Cambridge University Press 1966; E. Haenchen, *The Acts of the Apostles*, Blackwell 1971.

7 Who was St Peter?

No reader of the New Testament can fail to be aware that one of the most important figures in the gospels and the Acts of the Apostles is Peter. Church tradition credits this disciple with being the founder of the church in Rome and consequently the first bishop of Rome and first Pope.

If we can accept that the gospels tell us the historical facts about the period of Jesus' ministry, then the importance of Peter in Jesus' movement revealed there would explain why he became the leader of the Jerusalem church after Jesus' death as recorded in Acts and in Paul's letters. Few scholars, however, would accept that the gospels can be read in this way: most would argue that the gospels, which for the most part were written at least thirty years after the events they speak of, were in fact influenced by the teaching, events and presuppositions of the early Christian communities which produced them. This means that the gospels are more likely to state Peter was the foremost of the disciples *because* he had been leader of the Jerusalem church.

It is unlikely therefore that Peter became head of the church after the first Easter merely because of his earlier prominence in Jesus' ministry. Similarly, it is unlikely he became leader because Jesus had appointed him to this: passages in the New Testament gospels in which Jesus sets Peter up as the prime disciple are prophecies after the events.

Unfortunately there is a tantalizing gap between Jesus' death at the end of the gospels and the emergence of the church in Jerusalem as recorded in Acts and as recognized by Paul. We therefore do not know the steps whereby the disciples reassembled with Peter as their head to inaugurate the spread of the church in the name of Jesus. The gospels are probably correct in recording that the disciples forsook Jesus at the time of his arrest. There is no reason to assume that this detail was an invention by the evangelists in pursuit of an anti-Jerusalem church bias because the later gospels are all at pains to justify and explain why Jesus did die forsaken by his erstwhile colleagues. What we do not know is how and when the disciples met up again in Jerusalem. Mark and Matthew assume that the disciples had returned to the Galilee (Mark 16.7, Matt. 28.7) but the centre of the newly formed church began in Jerusalem according to Acts and Paul and it is in Jerusalem where Luke and John (1-20) set their post-resurrection appearances.

Possibly one reason for Peter's assumption of leadership was that he was the first one among Jesus' former colleagues to come to the belief that Jesus was raised from the dead, and that in the confidence of that belief he mustered the other disciples to continue Jesus' work. Resurrection belief involved the conviction that Jesus' movement and mission had not died with him. Peter therefore may well have been the first to encourage a reassembly of the disciples to continue to fight for the aims Jesus had died for. Certainly it is a strongly based tradition in the New Testament that the first of Jesus' post-resurrection appearances was to Peter. The earliest list of the appearances is in I Corinthians 15.5, which begins by recording an appearance to Kephas, the Aramaic form of Peter's name. The angelic messenger's proclamation in Mark 16.7 seems to suggest that Peter, independently of the other disciples, is to be granted an appearance of the risen Jesus. Similarly Luke 24.34 at the conclusion of the account of the walk to Emmaus points out that the resurrection appearance to Cleopas and his companion was not the first, and that the risen Jesus had already appeared to Simon Peter.

It may be argued that the priority given to Peter in these post-Easter references is comparable to the primacy of Peter in the rest of the gospels, and that all the references to Peter's superiority are retrojections into the gospels of the situation in the life of the early Jerusalem church, when Peter was already a leader – but there is an interesting difference. Unlike the accounts of Peter in the ministry period, the references to the post-resurrection appearances are lacking in detail. It is in fact remarkable that despite this tradition that

Jesus' first resurrection appearance was to Peter, that appearance is merely echoed in the gospels and I Corinthians and is nowhere recorded in full. Unlike the other Easter stories, in which Jesus appears to the women, or to the eleven disciples collectively, or to the men on the way to Emmaus, no story about Peter's alleged confrontation with Jesus is either invented or remembered. If there ever had been such a story it was certainly suppressed or forgotten by the time the gospels were composed. All that remains is the basis for the tradition.

It is an interesting speculation whether such a resurrection story had originally formed the climax to Mark's gospel in those verses subsequent to Mark 16.8, which is the ending to the gospel as we now have it. Those extant manuscripts which have conclusions beyond this point give non-Markan compositions. Mark 16.7 certainly anticipates an appearance to Peter and it is an anticlimax to find that Mark's gospel suddenly concludes at the following verse without recording this appearance. If the genuine, original, ending to Mark's gospel did in fact contain such an appearance to Peter it may have been excised precisely because it contained this appearance. A reason why this could have happened will be offered below. All we can say now is that the tradition if not the details of Jesus' first resurrection appearance is well established and may well give us the historical basis for Peter's rise to power after Jesus' death.

Peter on this argument became the first leader of the Christian church not because of his prominence among the disciples during Jesus' lifetime or because Jesus nominated him for such a role but because it was believed – no doubt due to Peter's publicizing his own conviction – that Jesus appeared to him first after the crucifixion.

I

Peter's original name was Simon, or Symeon to use the semitic form found on James' lips at Acts 15.14. According to Matthew 16.17 he was Simon baryona. This might mean he was Simon son of Jonah or, as interpreted in John 1.42 and 21.15f. son of John, or that he was a zealot: some lexicographers connect the word 'baryona' with the word for terrorist. If the latter is correct then this disciple would have been in good company with Simon the Zealot, Judas Iscariot (which may mean 'assassin') and the 'sons of thunder', James and John.

The reason why Simon was nicknamed Peter (meaning 'a rock') is given in Matthew 16.16b–19 where it is stated that Simon is to be the foundation-rock of the church. Peter is the Greek for the Aramaic Kephas, a form of the name which is transliterated rather than translated in some parts of the New Testament, but neither Kephas nor Peter was a personal name until Simon the disciple was so named. Strictly speaking therefore we should speak of this apostle as Simon Rock if we are to preserve the shock and significance of the nickname.

The gospels are not agreed as to the point in Jesus' ministry when Simon received this soubriquet. Matthew as we have seen places it in chapter 16 at the time of the confession at Caesarea Philippi. Earlier in the gospel Matthew speaks of 'Simon called Peter' at 4.18, thus anticipating the naming ceremony, and also at 10.2, when the twelve disciples are chosen. The latter parallels Mark 3.16 and Luke 6.14 which is where these gospels describe the renaming, suggesting that in the original traditions about Jesus' ministry the explanation of Simon's renaming was at the time of the call of the twelve and that Matthew 16.16–18 represents a later development of the tradition.

The Fourth Gospel places the episode of the renaming earlier than the synoptic gospels, namely at the time of Simon's first meeting with Jesus (John 1.40–42). This is the only occurrence in John 1–20 of the name 'Simon' alone. Once named he is called 'Simon Peter' at first mention in each new story, and 'Peter' thereafter.

Mark tells of some stories involving Simon before the name Peter is given. When Jesus first meets him at 1.16 he is called Simon and the adjoining stories continue to call him by that name (1.29, 30, 36) until he is renamed at the time of the call of the twelve in 3.16. Mark therefore seems to be alert to the fact that to call him 'Peter' before 3.16 is anachronistic. After that point the name Peter is used consistently. Only at 14.37 in the story of the arrest in the garden of Gethsemane is Peter addressed by Jesus as Simon. It is plain that the vocative has been added here by Mark to the original tradition underlying this saying in so far as the second person plural is the form of the verbs following. The name is absent from the parallel in Luke 22.46 where Jesus addresses the disciples *en bloc*. In the Matthaean parallel Peter is addressed but not named in the saying. The normal tendency in the development of the gospel tradition was to add personal names to make indefinite groups definite and here Mark's account is likely to have an addition to an earlier, probably pre-literary, form of the saying. The addition in Mark seems to have come from a source which did not know Peter by this name. It is too subtle to suggest that Jesus avoided calling Peter by his nickname here because in this episode he is not betraying rocklike qualities. The Lucan parallel here seems to have removed the specific address to Peter because, as we shall demonstrate later, the later gospels and Luke in particular tended to avoid disparaging references to Peter.

Luke, like Mark, generally reserves 'Simon' for the period before the renaming. After this renaming at the time of the call of the twelve (Luke 6.14) 'Peter' is the usual appellation. However, in the prophecy of Peter's denial, peculiar to Luke at 22.31, Peter is addressed twice by Jesus as 'Simon'. As in Mark 14.37 it is likely that the original saying was addressed to the disciples in general insofar as the second person plural pronoun follows the vocatives, but that as the story developed in the pre-literary stage the name of the prime disciple was added. Another unique reference to Peter occurs in Luke at 24.34 and again Peter is known only as 'Simon'. It is interest-ing to speculate why some of these peculiar references to Peter know him as Simon, and thus spoil the symmetry and plan of the gospel as a whole. The most reasonable deduction is that the addition of the name Simon came into the individual stories at a time when they had already reached a fairly developed stage in their composition in the belief that Jesus only used this name when addressing Peter.

Matthew is less scrupulous in writing the name Peter before the connection with Simon is explained. As we have already seen, Matthew places the episode of the renaming in chapter 16 even though 10.2 seems to agree with the Markan and Lucan parallels. These references indicate that even Matthew was aware of the tradi-tion that Peter obtained this name at an earlier stage in Jesus' ministry. At Matthew 8.14 the name Peter occurs even though the parallels prefer to preserve the name Simon for this point in his career, and at Matthew 14.28–29 and 15.15 the name Peter occurs, again anachronistically. Once he is named 'Peter' in Matthew 16.18

Matthew like his synoptic colleagues calls the disciple by his sou-briquet, but, as in Mark 14.37 and Luke 22.31 the vocative 'Simon' occurs in speech later (at Matt. 17.25). The tradition that Jesus is believed to have addressed Peter by his original name seems to have reached the authors of these gospels independently, and each has added it to different speeches attributed to Jesus.

Acts as we might expect uses the name Peter consistently, but in the story of Peter and Cornelius (Acts 10.1–11.18) which we shall be arguing below to have come from a different source than the sur-rounding material, he is named as 'Simon called Peter' four times.

As far as Paul is concerned he prefers the Aramaic form of Peter's name, Kephas, and this may have special significance. Paul is the only author in the New Testament writing contemporaneously with Peter's leadership of the church in Palestine. The Acts of the Apostles covers the period of Paul's writings but is itself of much later date, and written from a different standpoint from Paul's. Whereas Acts is determined by and large to show the amicable and orderly progres-sion of Christianity from its apostolic origins in Jerusalem to the expanding gentile-dominated church centred in Rome, the insights Paul himself gives in his epistles into the actual events as opposed to the later idealized accounts of them in Acts are illuminating. This is especially true as regards Peter, and may indeed help us to under-stand Paul's predeliction for the older Aramaic form of Peter's nickname.

Paul was unable to ignore the position of Peter or of the Jerusalem church for the development of Christianity, and in fact he maintained his contact with that church as his main link with the Jesus of Nazareth whom he, Paul, is unlikely ever to have met or known. In the analogy of the olive trees in Romans 11 Paul shows that, as a Jew, he was conscious that the gentile Christian converts, to whom he set himself up as prime missioner, owed their traditions and historical roots to the Judaism of which Jesus is seen to be the end and fulfilment. Much of Paul's inferiority complex, revealed in the letters in his frequent self-justification that he is as good an apostle as Peter, is due to the facts first that, unlike Peter, he was not a disciple of the earthly Jesus, and secondly that at the beginning of the church he was a violent opponent of the Christian movement. For these reasons Paul maintained his contact with the Jerusalem church, and, according to the likeliest translation of Galatians 1.18, used Peter as a source of information, probably about the earthly Jesus.

However independent Paul's movement was or at least tried to be, and however divorced the gentile church eventually became from the foundation church in Jerusalem, the links with that church through either personal contacts or the financial contributions collected among the Pauline churches for the poor in Jerusalem were deliberately maintained. Even when the Jerusalem church disappeared at the time of the overthrow of the Temple in AD 70 these links were not forgotten as Acts, written towards the end of the century, clearly demonstrates. The historical links with Jesus of Nazareth personified in Peter and others in the Jerusalem church at the time of that church's existence were also preserved after its disappearance in the written gospels, which were possibly composed in the first instance to encapsulate the living traditions. According to the consensus of scholarly opinion, three of the gospels (Matthew, Luke and John) were compiled after AD 70, when the Jerusalem church was overthrown together with the temple.

Paul, like the evangelists later, needed to maintain that continuity with the historical Jesus which he felt was crucial, but his personal contacts with those who knew Jesus were hardly warm and affectionate. What he has to say about the Jerusalem church, and Peter in particular, reveals Peter in a light different from that shown in Acts, but in a way consistent with what is said about Peter in Mark's gospel in particular. It is very significant that Paul, almost exclusively in the New Testament, prefers to call Peter 'Kephas'. Of the ten references to this disciple by name in Paul's extant letters, only two call him Peter. The rest name him as Kephas as if to emphasize that he belongs to the semitic, pro-Jewish, branch of the church with which Paul was so regularly at loggerheads.

The animosity between Paul and the Jerusalem church leaders is particularly apparent in Galatians 2. Peter here, and James and John, are referred to sarcastically as 'pillars of the church' and as 'people who are reputed to be of significance'. In fact, in reading this chapter the repeated 'reputed to be something' recalls Mark Anthony's repeated reference to Brutus as an 'honourable man' in Shakespeare's *Julius Caesar* Act III, scene II.

Although Paul is under an obligation to recognize the authority and unique standing of the church leaders in Jerusalem he does not approve of their limiting Christianity to Judaism. They are the missioners to the Jews, he to the gentiles, and he refuses to bow to their strictures on the liberty he adopts in his evangelizing. Galatians 2 probably refers to Paul's visit to Jerusalem recorded in Acts 15 in the context of the Council of Jerusalem. If so there are many significant changes made by the author of Acts in order to maintain his theological aim of smoothing over the differences between the two branches of the early church, pro-gentile and pro-Jewish. Acts reports that at this Council some minimal, mainly ritual, requirements of Jewish law were to be exacted of gentile converts to Christianity, but Paul in Galatians 2 knows of no such curb on his freedom, and in the rest of his letters gives us no clue that the precepts of the Council as listed in Acts 15.29 affected his later decisions about such matters as food regulations in I Corinthians or Romans.

Similarly Galatians 2 implies that Paul's companion Timothy had not been circumcized on becoming a Christian: Acts 16.3 implies Paul conformed to the Jerusalem church's insistence that the gentile Timothy had to be circumcized. Likewise in Acts 21.18 Paul is said to report to the Jerusalem church leaders and account for his gentile mission and to submit to purification in the temple. This ritual is yet another indication in Acts that Paul and the Jerusalem leaders are not so different from one another. Paul is here shown to be a loyal Jew but behind this story the differing ideals of both branches of the church are barely concealed. If this subjugation of Paul to James is historical then Paul himself does not choose to allude to this denial of his right to be free of the Torah in any of his extant writings. These contradictions between Paul and Acts indicate that, however polemical Paul's attitude, his version of events written as it were in the immediacy of the moment is a more reliable guide than the views expressed in Acts written probably more than forty years later at a time when the heat of the situation had gone.

As Galatians 2 continues in verses 11–14 Paul tells us how at Antioch he opposed Kephas to his face for lacking in principle and for being over-influenced by the 'advocates of circumcision', that is the stricter colleagues in Jerusalem.

Paul's references to Peter and the Jerusalem church in other letters are no more cordial. What is important to note though is that whether Paul was writing to the church in Galatia, or in Corinth, he assumes his readers know Peter and what he stands for. Acts tells us little of Peter's missionary activity, and nothing of Peter in Corinth or Galatia, but I Corinthians suggests that Peter had been to Corinth, insofar as the Corinthians seem to be aware that Peter travels with his wife. What is probably of greater importance is that in I Corinthians 1.12 Paul refers to the divisions in this nascent church between those who claim allegiance to Paul, and those who belong to Apollos or to Kephas. These factions are possibly rival parties among the Corinthians depending on which preacher's teaching they followed. Paul, characteristically, refuses to acknowledge that Kephas has any more importance, especially in Corinth (a church founded by Paul), than Paul himself (I Cor. 3.22). Paul argues against the schism and against the attempts made by others to win the Corinthian Christians over to their predominantly anti-Pauline cause. At I Corinthians 3.10 Paul reminds his readers that he founded their church but warns that 'someone else is putting up the building' and that this workmanship will have to be tested in the last judgment. This contrasts with Romans 15.20 in a letter sent to a church not founded by Paul when Paul claims he does not wish to build on 'another man's' foundations. In both these verses it is not unreasonable to deduce that this mysterious 'other man' was in fact Peter. Veiled allusions and threats of this sort recur in II Corinthians 10.7 where Paul claims to be as much a Christian as 'someone else'; and at II Corinthians 11.4–5 where he describes the 'someone else' who preaches 'another Jesus not the Jesus whom we proclaimed' as 'one of the superlative apostles'. This recalls the 'men of repute' in Galatians 2 and their perversion of the pro-gentile message preached by Paul in opposition to the 'different' gospel castigated in Galatians 1.6–9. These references to those who pervert Paul's message or to Judaizers or to those who make Paul's life difficult would fit the Jerusalem church establishment, whose most vehement denunciation occurs in Philippians 3.

II

Reference has already been made to the softening of Peter's role by the author of Acts. This is partly the result of the author's attempt to show how similar Peter was to Paul or rather Paul to Peter. Paul is consistently shown to be as good an apostle as Peter – and in many respects, the true successor to Peter as the main Christian evangelizer and missionary. In the previous chapter I tried to indicate the main theological tendencies at work in Acts. One of these is the attempt to remove the differences between the two leading protagonists in the early church. Actions, speeches and attributes of one man are transferred to the other. The author, writing from a pro-Pauline angle, attempted to rehabilitate Paul in the minds of readers whose church may well have been inclined to promote the memory of Peter, so that by robbing Peter to pay Paul the author has in effect diminished Peter's unique role in a far more subtle way than Paul himself did in his letters. Both Paul himself and the author of Acts have similar aims, even if both have different styles and approach, and these are to reduce the standing of Peter, as representing the Jerusalem church, and argue for the validity of the gentile church.

This perhaps is not so obvious from the early chapters in Acts but is increasingly apparent once Paul begins to dominate the book. The basic picture of Peter at the beginning of Acts is that he and the Jerusalem church carried on where Jesus left off, and that there is an organic growth from Jesus to the church. Whereas the disciples are said to be powerless to perform miracles in Jesus' lifetime (Matt. 17.16), in Acts Peter is a miracle worker and one who can raise the dead just like his master. Unlike the Peter of the ministry period, Peter the church leader in Acts has the authority to preach and teach in the name of Jesus. He is consistently shown to be in receipt of divine guidance. But in at least two places in Acts he seems not to have had overriding authority: at Acts 8.14 he is commanded by others, and at 11.1–4 he has to explain himself to the rest of the church. These suggest that Peter's authority was not so dominant as the author of Acts wished to convey in the rest of these early chapters. That is partly because he was concerned not so much to retell the actual historic conditions of the earliest church, but merely to focus on Peter as an example or personification of that early Jerusalem-based church.

The experiences of Peter and by extension the earliest Christians were read back not only into the gospels' accounts of for instance the sending out of the twelve, and the seventy-two (Luke 9 and 10) but also into these accounts of the early church in Acts. The climax to

Matthew's and Luke's gospels has the risen Jesus inaugurate the church and command the disciples to do what the author of Acts tries to dramatize. All are based on what was remembered of the life of that formative church. The early Christians and Peter in particular are thus shown in Acts to be acting in imitation of Jesus under the guidance of his spirit, and this has influenced how Acts speaks of Peter.

By writing in this way the author of Acts has falsified the actual state of affairs in a way one suspects Paul himself did not. For instance Peter in Acts is shown to have indulged in at least a token missionary activity among gentiles. The story of the conversion of Cornelius in Acts 10–11 may well be yet another story in which Peter and Paul are shown to be similar. This story (which possibly reached the author from a different source from the surrounding material) seems to have been designed to show to readers prejudiced in favour of the pro-Petrine point of view that Paul's gentile missionary activity had its precedent in the conversion by Peter of a Roman citizen. Thus Paul's subsequent behaviour was 'approved' and made respectable.

The need to fight for the existence of a pro-gentile mission is one of the main motives behind the writing of Acts insofar as the gentile mission is said to have started, albeit tentatively, with Peter, before being successfully carried out by Paul. Even if Jesus did intend to found a church (and not all theologians would accept that he did) it is unlikely he intended a gentile mission. Sayings such as 'Do not take the road to gentile lands . . . but go rather to the lost sheep of the house of Israel' (Matt. 10.5–6) and 'Do not give dogs (= gentiles) what is holy; do not feed your pearls to pigs (= gentiles)' (Matt. 7.6) and the refusal of Jesus to take the children of Israel's bread and throw it to the dogs in the story of the Syrophoenician (or Canaanite) woman's daughter (Matt. 15.26 and Mark 7.28) show that these pro-Jewish slogans originating if not with Jesus at least in the Jerusalem church were remembered and attributed to Jesus as being consonant with his own aims. If Jesus had in fact intended a pro-gentile mission it is improbable that Paul would have met such hostility to his mission or that those pro-Jewish sayings would have become associated with Jesus himself.

Acts may attempt to conceal any distinction between Paul and Peter with the purpose of enhancing Paul's standing in the church at large, but Acts reveals despite itself a different sort of rivalry, that is the power struggle among the leaders of the Jerusalem church. Although Peter is the founder church leader and prominant as such up to the point reached in Acts 12, he is then suddenly written out of the book with the words 'he left the house and went off elsewhere'. Inevitably commentators have speculated where 'elsewhere' is likely to have been, and if the author deliberately suppressed the information for reasons best known to himself and best suited to his subtly pro-Pauline bias. What is significant is that immediately prior to these words, the author makes Peter refer to 'James and the brothers' whereas in the early chapters the author refers to Peter as the leader of the church brethren. What begins at Acts 2.37 as 'Peter and the apostles' becomes 'the apostles and elders in Jerusalem' in Acts 16.4 and 'James and the elders' in 21.18. It is as if the author of Acts was aware that at a certain point in the history of the primitive church, the leadership in Jerusalem passed from Peter to James.

Again Acts has a tantilizing gap for our knowledge of what precisely happened. It is possible that Peter was taking too soft a line with Paul over the pro-gentile movement. This theory can be substantiated even if we do not accept the historicity of the Cornelius episode. Acts records the Council of Jerusalem: Peter reappears here for the last time and in his swansong urges leniency towards Paul. As the Council is reported, Peter's argument is ignored and it is James the new leader of the church who is remembered as insisting on a stronger reaction to Paul and it is James' more rigorous pro-Jewish line which is followed. The Council concludes with the Jerusalem establishment commanding that James' views be communicated to certain churches in Antioch, Syria and Cilicia. The author of Acts was perhaps aware that some mixed Jewish and non-Jewish churches in the areas mentioned there abided by the regulations given in Acts 15.29 and that they claimed this teaching was apostolic in origin. One needs to be alert to the possibility that Acts in its desire to bridge the gap between the two branches of the church has softened its references not only to Peter but to James as well. Nevertheless James appears as more rigorous than Peter in Acts. In point of fact this impression is in line with Paul's own account. At Galatians 2.11–14 Paul recalls that Peter's apparent willingness to eat with gentile Christians was curtailed by 'certain persons sent by James'.

Another indication of James' hard-line pro-Jewishness may be seen in the epistle which bears his name in the New Testament canon. The three pillars of the church in Jerusalem are listed by Paul in Galatians 2 as Peter, James and John. Each seems to have had adherents in the later years of the first century who perpetuated his teaching and memory. Just as we have letters written in Paul's name (such as I and II Timothy and Titus for example) by followers of his style of teaching, so too letters were composed in the names of Peter, John and also James. We shall refer below to the pseudonymous epistles of Peter but here it is relevant to indicate that the Epistle of James, albeit pseudonymous in the view of the majority of biblical exegetes, is nevertheless in line with the strong pro-Jewish line associated in church tradition with James the brother of Jesus, and its contents entirely consistent with those Christians who were determined to perpetuate the wing of the church personified by James. The epistle not surprisingly betrays an anti-Pauline stand (just as II Peter does). James 2.14–26, for instance, emphasizes justification by good works and this seems to run counter to Paul's teaching on justification by faith alone.

If Peter's standing in the church was due to his having claimed to be the first to see the risen Christ, James no doubt claimed his authority by virtue of his being Jesus' brother (Gal. 1.19). Acts 1.14 retails the tradition that even at the beginning of the church in Jerusalem Jesus' mother and brothers were actively involved.

This kinship was however not sufficient, and so the tradition developed that claimed that James like Peter had also been privy to a post-resurrection appearance. The list of those granted Christophanies appears in I Corinthians 15.3–7 and has already been referred to above with reference to Peter. This list is stated by Paul there to have been received from Christian tradition. Paul's main contribution to the list is likely to have been only the addition of his own name at the end of the list to demonstrate that he was of a similar standing to the other apostles, having had a similar experience to theirs. Some scholars have suggested that originally the list received by Paul was in two parts (15.5–6 and 15.7). The first list starts with Kephas and includes appearances to the twelve disciples, then to the five hundred plus. The second represents a rival list which was prepared in order to place James at the head, and follow this with the appearance to the other apostles. Be that as it may, the fact remains that the only two individuals who are reported in that earliest tradition to have seen the risen Jesus are the two men who became leaders of the Jerusalem church. It is with that tradition that Paul tries to claim equality. It seems probable therefore that the power struggle for leadership in the early church resulted in James' assumption of leadership sometime before the Council of Jerusalem is said to have taken place and the subsequent ousting of Peter. Having replaced Peter, James, because of his kinship and his stricter adherence to the pro-Jewish question, is then credited with having had a resurrection appearance too. The canonical gospels do not record this appearance to James although the apocryphal *Gospel to the Hebrews* perpetuates a tradition, probably originating among the adherents of James' movement in which the *first* post-resurrection appearance is assigned not to Peter but to James. The rivalry at the apex of the Jerusalem church's establishment seems therefore to have been kept alive long after the original protagonists had left the scene.

The perpetuation of this rivalry may also be seen in the textual tradition of the Greek New Testament manuscripts. It was hinted at earlier that an anti-Petrine movement may have been responsible for depriving Mark's gospel of its original ending. Subsequent tampering with the New Testament documents is more demonstrable in two other places. At Galatians 2.9 modern texts normally print the names of the pillars of the church in the order James followed by Kephas, but many New Testament manuscripts either have a different order with James second or else omit the reference to Kephas. (John here remains fixed in the tradition as the last named). Whatever order we would wish to argue on text-critical grounds to be the original, it is obvious that at a date subsequent to the original composition, scribes were prepared to adjust the text they were copying. That these changes were due either to an anti-Petrine or an anti-James tendency in the communities, in which these variants were first introduced, cannot be ruled out.

A similar phenomenon can be detected at Luke 24.12. This verse tells of Peter's visit to the tomb on Easter day. The verse is absent from some early manuscripts. If original to Luke its deletion could again be due to an anti-Petrine tendency on the part of the scribe or the community in which he worked; if secondary then its addition to

Luke (possibly as a digest of the parallel account in John 20.2–10) was motivated by the opposite tendency—namely a desire to exalt Peter.

All that may be said with confidence about these textual problems is that the primacy of Peter was an issue which continued to be controversial even after the New Testament books had been composed and that this controversy caused scribes to tamper with the text. The pro- and anti-Petrine tendencies however had their roots in the gospel tradition itself, and it is this which must next be examined.

We have already seen that Paul is strongly anti-Peter, whereas Acts, although giving us some interesting insights into the status of the earliest Christian community in Jerusalem, tries by and large to minimize the differences between Peter and Paul. With this knowledge, it is necessary now to examine how Peter is treated in the three synoptic gospels (Matthew, Mark, Luke) which, it is usually conceded, were written in the period between the letters of Paul and the composition of Acts. These gospels are likely to have been compiled in churches influenced, in some cases directly, by Paul's own teaching, and this probability may account for any Pauline traits in the way the gospels speak of Peter. But the gospels are intermediate between Paul and Acts, and as Acts is volume two of Luke–Acts it is important to recognize that the way Acts writes about Peter would be influenced by the way the gospels (or Luke in particular) portrayed him.

If we take Mark first as the gospel standing closest in time to Paul it is significant how the strongly anti-Petrine tone used by Paul has permeated this gospel. The attitude of the gentile church towards Peter in the ministry of the early church has influenced Mark's telling of Peter in the ministry of Jesus. This hostility is evidenced in those stories which emphasize Peter's failings, his impulsiveness, lack of understanding and ignorance. This anti-Petrine bias so characteristic of Mark's gospel reaches its climax in the stories of the denial. At a time when all the disciples are said to have fled, Mark brings Peter back into the scene of Jesus' questioning before the Sanhedrin in order to focus more specifically on what deserting Jesus meant in the case of the main representative of the twelve disciples. The scene also provides a dramatic juxtaposition of stories. Jesus acts in a dignified courageous manner before the high priest whereas

Peter outside in the courtyard acts in a cowardly undignified manner during his questionings by the high priest's servant. Peter's final appearance in Mark is when he curses Jesus (14.71 – not in the parallels) and breaks down weeping after the threefold denial of association with Jesus.

Another example in this gospel which shows how the early pro-gentile branch of the church regarded Peter may be seen in the story of the confession at Caesarea Philippi (8.27–33). Here Peter acknowledges Jesus as Messiah, a title which Mark underplays as it could be an inadequate and limiting title liable to be understood to refer to a pro-Jewish or nationalist figure.

Mark, in particular, prefers to use the title 'Son of God' of Jesus. It is significant that the twofold title used in the first verse of this gospel describes Jesus the Messiah as Son of God. It is this second title which forms the climax to the gospel at the point of Jesus' death. It is remarkable that Peter uses the pro-Jewish and less acceptable title, Messiah, at Caesarea Philippi and even more significant for Mark's pro-Pauline theology that it is a Roman centurian at the foot of the cross who is made to confess Jesus immediately after his death by the title which the pro-gentile church preferred. Peter in this story is therefore shown to have an inadequate vision of Jesus' role, and also of his mission: and Peter is made to represent a view that denies to Jesus the essential Christian ingredient of suffering. It is for this that Mark makes Jesus pronounce Peter to be Satan. This damning of Peter by Jesus is avoided in the later gospels of Luke and John.

The early Christian writer Papias in a famous passage claims Mark to be Peter's interpreter. That tradition is true only insofar as Mark interprets the role of Peter in the judgment of the gentile church.

A further derogatory reference to Peter interpreting him in this way occurs at another poignant moment in Jesus' career, namely the agony in Gethsemane. Here in Mark 14.37 it is Peter who is addressed by Jesus as being unable to stay awake to share in Christ's vigil. Although this reference is retained by Matthew, Luke avoids mentioning Peter here. This scene in Mark anticipates the final desertion of Jesus by the twelve in general and by Peter in particular, and is typical of this gospel which denigrates all the disciples because they formed the nucleus of the Jerusalem church later.

The desertion by the disciples at the time of Jesus' arrest, and the treachery of Judas are unlikely to have been invented but these stories of failure were remembered and retold by Mark as symptomatic of the behaviour of the earliest close followers of Jesus. The later gospels try to find theological explanations why Peter, Judas, and the twelve in general behaved as they did. Such apologies are absent from Mark's stark account.

But just as Mark is hostile to Peter and the twelve, he is equally hostile to James and the family of Jesus, for these too formed the basis of the Jerusalem church hierarchy. As we saw in Chapter 3, it is significant how little part Jesus' siblings or family play in the gospels – especially when we consider James' rise to power in the period after Jesus' crucifixion. What Mark does tell us is unflattering. At 6.1–6 Jesus is made to claim that he is dishonoured by his family, and at 3.31–35 Jesus' brothers and mother are literally, and metaphorically, outsiders, and here Jesus is made to say that his real family are those who do God's will. (A similar motive to denigrate the family of Jesus is found in the Fourth Gospel where John 7.5 tells us that Jesus' brothers 'did not believe in him', and may also be detected in Luke's gospel (14.26) in that difficult saying in which Jesus is represented as refusing to accept as his followers those who do not hate their siblings and parents.)

In other parts of his gospel Mark preserves the traditional stories about Peter which he received from the earliest pre-Pauline days of the church when Peter was unquestionably the leading apostle. The healing of Peter's mother-in-law, or those stories in which Peter acts as spokesman for the disciples probably originated in the Jerusalem church. Other stories place Peter and the sons of Zebedee as an inner core of disciples present at such events as the healing of Jairus' daughter, at the transfiguration, and when Jesus prepares for Gethsemane (14.32–33).

The determination to make Peter the prime disciple is evidenced by comparing the gospels whenever they tell the same story. The alteration of an indefinite group to a definite is a characteristic in the development of the gospel material in the course of both the oral and written transmission as has already been indicated. Further examples may be seen at Luke 12.41 where Jesus' further comments are the result of Peter's question: in the earlier gospel of Matthew Jesus addresses 'the disciples' (24.45). In the story of the woman with the haemorrhage at Mark 5.31 the disciples speak: the Lukan parallel (8.45) makes Peter the spokesman. Whereas Mark and Matthew have 'disciples' sent to prepare the passover Luke specifies these as Peter and John, that is two of the pillars of the Jerusalem church who are to figure later in his second volume at Acts 3.1ff.; 4.13ff.; 8.14. But because of the polemical nature of the writing about Peter this tendency to add the name Peter is not carried out in an automatic way. Sometimes only the earliest gospel has the name Peter and the later gospels have expunged it in order to avoid a derogatory reference. We have already noted this above at Mark 8.33 and 14.37 when these verses are compared to the parallels in Luke.

Similarly at Luke 17.1–4 Jesus speaks to 'the disciples': the parallel to this in the earlier gospel of Matthew (18.22) has Jesus replying to Peter. Also, at Mark 13.3 the apocalyptic discourse results from a question put to Jesus by four disciples led by Peter: in Matthew 24.3 he addresses the disciples en bloc, and in Luke 21.7 his questioners are unnamed. A final example may be pointed to at Matthew 21.20 where it is the disciples who speak about the fig-tree: at Mark 11.21 only Peter makes the comment.

However, even though we can demonstrate that on occasion the later gospels avoid mentioning Peter by name this was usually done to avoid a critical reference to Peter made in the earlier gospel, and in general the tendency was to increase the number of favourable references to Peter in direct proportion to the increasing adulation of that prime disciple. This growing devotion to the memory of Peter becomes evident the further we move away from the Pauline-influenced gospel of Mark, and closer to the composition of Acts.

As far as Matthew is concerned, although he preserves several of Mark's derogatory references to Jesus' family, the disciples and Peter, it is in this gospel that some of the most honorific references to Peter occur. Matthew, unlike Luke, keeps faithfully to much of the material he found in his Markan source, but, like Luke Matthew wrote after AD 70 when the Jerusalem church had been destroyed along with the Jewish temple. This event affected the later writers' judgment on the Jerusalem church. Whereas Mark and Paul were writing at a time when the Jerusalem church was still exercising its often restrictive influence, after 70 the gentile church was the dominant wing of Christianity. Hence those founder disciples tended to be viewed no longer as an immediate threat, but remembered as a cherished link with Jesus of Nazareth. This might explain why once Peter and the Jerusalem church ceased to exist and were no longer a bridle on the gentile mission, these early Christians were thought of not so much as church leaders but as erstwhile companions of Jesus.

Although Matthew keeps references such as Peter's vehement affirmation in 26.35 (taken from Mark) that he will not desert Jesus, he has sometimes added details about Peter to Mark's account, and these are instructive. At 15.15 it is Peter who asks Jesus for the meaning of the parable just related, and is rebuked for being as dull as the rest of the disciples. In this Matthew is close to Mark and it is significant to note that when Peter as spokesman makes a similar request for the interpretation of a parable in a different context at Luke 12.41 Jesus there answers Peter without any rebuke. But Matthew nevertheless can be seen to be moving away from Mark towards the stand taken by Luke regarding the twelve. At Matthew 18.21f. a more favourable reference to Peter occurs, when Peter as spokesman asks Jesus for an authoritative statement on the nature of Christian forgiveness. There is no hostility to Peter here.

Generally, it is the peculiar references to Peter in Matthew, rather than in his additions to Markan material, which give an enhanced view of Peter and show us Matthew's distinctive contribution to the rehabilitation of this disciple. These unique stories occur in Matthew 14.28–31; 16.16–19; 17.24–27 in that section of the gospel dealing with the church. Matthew 14.28–33 tells of Peter's attempt to walk on the water. This is the only place in the gospels where Jesus performs a miracle just for Peter. This story can be seen as an intermediate stage between Mark's stark portrayal of Peter the failure and the later idealized picture of him in Luke–Acts. Here Peter is rebuked by Jesus as a man of little faith but nevertheless it is Peter's action which gives the other disciples their faith and they confess Jesus as Son of God. There is thus an ambiguity in the scene and it seems as if Matthew working on material similar to that found in Mark's sources tried to find a favourable interpretation in a scene originally anti-Petrine.

A story in which there is no trace of an anti-Petrine tradition is Matthew 16.16b–19. This is Matthew's radical adaptation of the confession at Caesarea Philippi, in which Peter is made to confess not that Jesus is Messiah but that he is a Messiah reinterpreted as 'Son of the living God'. In this Peter repeats the confession recorded earlier at 14.33 where the disciples address Jesus in this way. What is more important for Matthew in this account of the confession by Peter is that it results in Jesus' proclamation of Peter's superiority. This represents the early Jerusalem church's belief that because Peter was their first leader then Jesus himself must have ordained it. Peter is given here his highest acclaim to be the foundation rock of Jesus' church. Although all the gospels agree that Jesus named Simon 'Peter' it is only here that the explanation of this nickname is preserved. It is in this passage also that Peter is blessed – the only disciple to be blessed in the whole of the New Testament. Peter alone is then told he will be given the 'keys to the kingdom of heaven' and the rest of the disciples are told that they will have power to bind and loose. These difficult sayings have inevitably been subjected to much investigation. The theological importance and significance of the sayings is best discussed elsewhere, but there is no denying the high estimate of Peter and the exalted role for the disciples in these verses. It is of course on these verses that the unique position of Peter as first Pope is usually justified. What is significant is that the language and style of this passage is very semitic in tone, which suggests that the sayings, even if not authentic to Jesus, certainly seem to reflect the language of the Jerusalem-based church. It is interesting that Matthew, twenty years later than Mark, felt able to incorporate in his gospel this old tradition.

It is unlikely that the sayings in Matthew 16.16–19 actually came from Jesus himself insofar as it is improbable that Jesus anticipated the founding of a church. This question is naturally much debated but on the basis of the New Testament his intentions are ambiguous. If Jesus did in fact intend the establishment of a church it is likely he saw it as a New Israel in which the twelve disciples would rule the twelve tribes (Matthew 19.28). As far as the remembrance of the sayings in Matthew 16 is concerned it seems as if Peter's eminence and importance apparent in this early tradition went through a period of reaction, initiated by Paul and reflected in his letters and in Mark, but by the time Matthew wrote there was an attempt to reappraise his real significance both in the life of Jesus and in the life of the church. Matthew in other words seems to reflect the early need to re-establish the apostolic links with the Jerusalem based church after 70. A similar motive may be seen below when we consider John 21.

Another story concerning Peter peculiar to Matthew's gospel is the episode of the temple tax in 17.24–27. The position of the Christians *vis à vis* the Roman state as exemplified in the individual's need to pay tax to Rome is evidenced not only in Romans 13 where civic obligations are enjoined on Christians, and in the dominical saying 'Render unto Caesar. . . .' in the gospels, but also in stories telling of Jesus' consorting with taxgatherers thus making them acceptable and 'respectable'. These together with this story in Matthew 17 were doubtless of apologetic importance in the early Christians' dealings with the Roman authorities on whose goodwill their existence depended. As with the other two Petrine stories unique to Matthew in the synoptic tradition noted above, this story of the half-shekel has its parallel in John 21 (the chapter in the Fourth Gospel most favourably disposed to Peter) insofar as the story here could be a Matthean adaptation of the account which reached John 21.9–13 (and possibly Luke 5.1–11 also) as the miraculous draft of fishes. As with Peter's walking on the water, the miracle as told in Matthew 17.24–27 is performed for the benefit of the miracle worker. It seems as if for Matthew's church it was relevant for Peter to be able to provide a Christian answer to questions about tax. Peter here has the authority to teach in the name of Jesus and to reply that 'God will provide'. Peter's role has thus come close to that assigned him in the early speeches in Acts.

Matthew's description of Peter as the prime disciple is clearest in 10.2 where, uniquely among the four lists of disciples given in the New Testament, Matthew adds the word 'first' to the choosing of Peter. For Matthew's community Peter is set apart from and is above the other disciples. The authority accorded him in this gospel came from Jesus' appointing him to be the leader of his church after the confession at Caesarea Philippi. This tradition therefore represents an evaluation of Peter's role in at least part of the church at that time, and it is a tradition maintained by Luke.

Having examined the treatment of Peter in Acts it is not surprising to find a similar portrayal of Peter in Luke's gospel. Luke has refined the Markan description of Peter even more than Matthew, and it is in this gospel that Peter is idealized. Luke avoids most of the derogatory designations of Peter. For example he deletes Jesus' rebuke of Peter after the confession. He also softens the references to Peter in the passion story. Similarly in the story of the woman with a haemorrhage (Luke 8.40–56) Luke has Peter gently point out the crowds thronging Jesus and this is in contrast to the more petulant comment of the disciples in the Markan parallel. In the predictions of the denials Luke adds at 22.31–34 the prophecy that Jesus is praying for Peter in his ordeal and that afterwards Peter will 'turn again and strengthen his brothers'. This is comparable to the rehabilitation of Peter in John 21 to be discussed below. Another link with John 21 already referred to is at Luke 5.1–11 which is a story unique to Luke in the synoptic tradition. Here Peter alone is given a personal call by Jesus and told he will be a fisher of men (even though two others are present in the story) unlike Matthew and Mark who have all the disciples described as fishers of men (Matt. 4.19; Mark 1.17).

In another incident unique to Luke (24.34) Jesus' appearance to Peter is recorded. It is the recording of the resurrection appearance to Peter that makes Peter the last named disciple in the gospel just as it is Peter who is the first disciple to be named in the second volume, Acts. In all these three episodes peculiar to Luke (5.1–11; 22.31–34; 24.34) it is significant that Peter is referred to by his original Jewish name Simon suggesting that these stories all came to Luke from a Palestinian source. (The name 'Peter' present in some manuscripts at 5.8 is unlikely to be original to the story.) These were used by Luke as being consonant with the image of Peter which he wished to preserve.

Despite the fact that the majority of scholars date the Fourth Gospel about AD 90 thus making it the last of the four gospels to be written, its treatment of Peter in chapters 1–20 is closer to Mark than Luke. The softening of Mark's anti-Petrine motif which we have traced through Matthew to Luke–Acts is not carried forward to the Fourth Gospel. The extent to which this gospel is independent of the synoptics is a crux of biblical scholarship but if the author of the Fourth Gospel really was unaware of the material as written in the synoptic gospels (especially outside the passion narrative) then he seems to have been aware of the traditions concerning Peter which find their place in Mark's gospel. However, unlike Mark, the Fourth

Gospel has a typically idiosyncractic way of dealing with the perfidy and inadequacies of Peter.

The Fourth Gospel tells of six stories concerning Peter which do not include his mysterious extra character, 'the beloved disciple'. Those which occur at John 1.40–42 (the call of Peter), 6.67–69 (the confession), 13.36–38 (Peter's inability to understand the significance of Jesus' words and the prediction of Peter's denials), and 18.25–27 (the denials) all have synoptic parallels. In addition the Fourth Gospel has two further stories concerning Peter without the beloved disciple, (13.6–11 and 18.10–11) which do not have synoptic parallels: both of these follow the Markan pattern and show Peter to be impulsive. Neither shows Peter in a favourable light. In the latter story the Fourth Gospel adds the detail that the previously unnamed person who cut off the servant's ear during the fracas in the garden of Gethsemane was in fact Peter. The story in chapter 13 which tells of the footwashing is an episode that replaces the institution of the Last Supper in this gospel and in many ways may be an allegory of the need for humility expressed more directly in the saying found at Luke 22.24–28 that no one disciple is to be deemed superior to another. In the footwashing episode it is Peter who is cast as the man most in need of humility.

Among the stories John has in common with the synoptics, it is significant to note that at 1.40–42 John tries to demote Peter from the assumption of priority. In his telling of the call it is not Peter who is the first to recognize Jesus, but, according to the most likely text here, Andrew. Nor is Peter the first disciple called. The other three stories repeat derogatory episodes known to the synoptics.

The remaining stories in the Fourth Gospel involving Peter also include the enigmatic beloved disciple. It has already been pointed out that elsewhere in the New Testament Peter is compared to and contrasted with Paul, and in other places is in apparent conflict with James. In the Fourth Gospel there is a further rivalry, this time between Peter and the beloved disciple. In the first of these stories (at the Last Supper) it is the beloved disciple who is accorded pride of place at Jesus' breast (John 13.23–26) and it is only through this mysterious disciple that Peter is able to find out from Jesus which of the twelve is to be the betrayer. The superior influence of this disciple is also seen in the story of the trials, when unlike Peter who has to wait outside the high priest's courtyard, 'another disciple', presumably the beloved disciple, has the authority to follow Jesus inside. It is only through this man's influence that Peter eventually gains access to the courtyard.

The superiority that this disciple is able to wield over Peter is also evidenced in the uniquely Johannine story at the cross when the dying Jesus entrusts his mother to the beloved disciple. This man is the only disciple not to have denied or deserted Jesus and is therefore unlike Peter who is absent when Jesus is, in the language of the Fourth Gospel, 'lifted up' in glory on to the cross.

By means of this regular comparison with the beloved disciple Peter's role is diminished and his relationship to Jesus distanced as it is evident that Peter is not the beloved disciple of Jesus – only among the most important of the *named* disciples, and even in this Peter does not predominate. Other disciples such as Thomas or Philip or Judas act as spokesmen (John 11.16; 14.5, 8, 22).

Another episode in which Peter and this disciple are contrasted to Peter's disadvantage is in the Easter story. Here in John 20.2–10 the beloved disciple and Peter race to Jesus' tomb. The beloved disciple outruns Peter, and when he subsequently follows Peter into the tomb 'he sees and believes' in the significance of the empty tomb, unlike Peter who merely looks. Other references to the beloved disciple occur in John 21, which needs to be treated as separated from chapters 1–20.

This Appendix to the Fourth Gospel has a different style and the theology is in some ways different from the bulk of the gospel to which it is attached. It is in this section that Peter is rehabilitated by having to confess his love for Jesus three times (John 21.15–17). This episode therefore provides an antidote to the earlier denials. As a result of the words of Peter, pastoral authority is laid on him by Jesus. Whereas John 1–20 betrays an attitude to Peter similar to Mark's or Paul's, chapter 21 seems to have been influenced by the growing veneration of Peter seen in Matthew and particularly in Luke–Acts. The Appendix may have been composed in the first instance in order to correct the image of Peter expressed in the first draft of the gospel (John 1–20).

John 21.1–14 follows the tradition found elsewhere at Luke 5.1–11 in which Peter is made to be the most important fisher of men. The author of this chapter has also reintroduced the beloved disciple and it is he rather than Peter who identifies Jesus on the shore as the Lord (John 21.7). John 21.7–8 may also have been influenced by the unique story in Matthew 14.8–31: in both Peter leaves the boat to go to Jesus despite an initial hesitation and in both Jesus is addressed by his resurrected title, 'Lord'.

Another function of the Appendix seems to have been to explain the destiny of both Peter and the beloved disciple. It is predicted here, doubtless with the wisdom of hindsight, not only how Peter is to die – apparently by crucifixion (if John 21.18 is to be taken literally) – but also that the beloved disciple himself was also to die although apparently not as a martyr. This statement concerning the beloved disciple was inserted to correct a mistaken belief in the Johannine circle that this disciple was destined to immortality. The Appendix also bears witness to the belief that the beloved disciple was the inspiration and authority behind John 21, and maybe chapters 1–20 as well, which no doubt explains why even in chapter 21 he is still depicted as superior to Peter.

Naturally enough, scholars have tried to identify this disciple who was present at among other events, the last supper, the crucifixion and at the empty tomb. His presence at the last supper suggests he was one of the twelve and John's oblique references to him throughout the Fourth Gospel imply that his readers knew who he was. Yet it is just as likely that John was referring to no one particular disciple but merely to an idealized form of discipleship. In contrast to the disgraced Peter of John 1–20 the beloved disciple is Peter's *alter ego* and as such the exemplary disciple which this gospel likes to promote in preference to the failing twelve.

III

It might be thought that the two letters of Peter in the New Testament canon would give a particularly intimate insight into the character of their author. Each probably does – but is unlikely to help us in our search for the historical St Peter. Most scholars doubt if the two letters bearing Peter's name were by the same author because the style, language and theology of both is so different. The consensus of academic opinion is that neither was written by Simon Peter. Several New Testament epistles were written in the name of a famous apostle. This was done not from a desire to deceive but in order to pay honour to the memory of a man whose views – supposed or actual – were being promulgated by his admirers and followers. In the case of the Petrine epistles it is obvious that some later Christians were prepared to honour Peter by composing letters in his name.

As far as I Peter is concerned it is interesting to note that this circular letter is addressed to churches with which Paul had also been associated. This suggests that Paul's presence in these communities had not succeeded in eliminating the outlook and influence of Peter. In the case of II Peter one of the purposes of the letter was to comment on the views of Paul and warn against unprincipled men who were apparently using Paul's words in a way the author disapproved of (II Peter 3.17). This letter is probably a fairly late composition and likely to be the latest in the canon to have been written: it assumes the existence of a Pauline corpus which in the eyes of the author was creating misinterpretation. The authority for the viewpoint in II Peter seems to have been St Peter's eyewitness and apostleship (II Peter 1.16–18).

These letters therefore do not tell us anything about the historical Peter, but they are powerful witnesses to a continuing dichotomy between Pauline and Petrine forces at work in the first-century church even at a time later than the composition of Luke–Acts with its intended palliative effect.

IV

Our survey of the biblical evidence about Peter shows his evident importance in the life of Jesus and the primitive church but also reveals the varying opinions and attitudes to him as his role was interpreted and remembered by later writers. The two most important traditions about Peter are his martyrdom and his being the first bishop of Rome. Yet these traditions cannot be read directly from the biblical evidence.

As we saw earlier, Acts tells us nothing about the founding of the church in Rome. All we know is that there was a Christian community there when Paul arrived. When Acts tells us Peter went off *elsewhere* the author could have been suppressing knowledge that the 'elsewhere' was in fact Rome, but this can only be guessed at. However it may be a deduction that can be substantiated.

The epistle to the Romans was sent by Paul early in his missionary career to a well-established church not founded by him. If Peter had founded that church, this may explain why Paul is so concerned in this letter above all to express his beliefs about God's purposes for gentiles and Jews and to clarify his own distinctive theological position to a church which in Paul's eyes had been based on a perverted view of the gospel. A similar need to correct Peter's teaching may have lain behind the composition of Mark's gospel which is of Roman provenence and written about the time Paul was in Rome.

A further claim that could help sustain the traditional linking of Peter with Rome is found in I Peter. Even if this letter was pseudonymous it emanated from a section of the church which venerated Peter. The letter claims to be sent from Babylon (I Peter 5.13) thought by many – probably correctly – to be a euphemism for Rome.

It is therefore possible to elicit some biblical support for the tradition that Peter was the founder of the church in Rome, but what of his alleged martyrdom? As we have already indicated, Peter's death by crucifixion is possibly predicted in John 21.18. Another New Testament indication that Peter was venerated as a martyr figure may be seen in I Peter, which is a letter written to give comfort and encouragement to Christians about to experience persecution. Such Christians could well have found a letter in Peter's name exemplary.

However, the tradition of Peter's martyrdom in Rome is not firmly stated in extant documentary evidence until the second half of the second century although there are one or two allusions in the earlier *I Clement* and Ignatius of Antioch's letters to Rome. Prior to the second century early Christian writers are silent about Peter's death.

The archaeological evidence which seeks to identify some bones buried under St Peter's in the Vatican as those of Simon Peter is inconclusive, and the real 'proof' for Peter's martyrdom in Rome must still be sought from literary evidence.

Peter as first Pope may be difficult to prove because the connexion with Rome is dubious. He was obviously the first leader of the Jerusalem church but because of his special history his authority was greater than that of just a local church leader. He certainly seems to have had an influence over churches founded by other Christians, although I Peter 5.1 remembers him as only as one elder among others. Peter as leader and spokesman of the twelve in the gospels; Peter as Jesus' choice to be the foundation stone of his church; the pastoral commission bestowed on Peter by the risen Jesus in John 21 are all pointed to by defenders of the church's tradition but if it is accepted that these sayings are creations of the early Jerusalem church in the light of Peter's assumption of leadership there, then the sayings cannot be used as divine commands regarding Peter's prominence.

The church tradition nevertheless may be historically accurate in stating that Peter was the leader of the church in Rome before his martyrdom but the biblical basis for this tradition is inconclusive. The later career and ultimate fate of Peter are not recorded in the New Testament. This may be because even these parts of the New Testament most favourably disposed to Peter are working from sources contaminated at an early date by the pervading influences of Paul and his anti-Petrine teaching. An attempt was begun in New Testament times to review Peter's career and rehabilitate him but the process was never completed in the first century. Vital early evidence once suppressed was doomed never to resurface. Apologists in later centuries may have tried to tap memories but for the most part the deeds of the historical Peter had been forgotten. Only the biblical evidence gets us close to the real man but even this is woefully inadequate and needs to be carefully sifted if any factual evidence is to be found in it.

Texts

Matthew 16.13–20; Mark 14.66–72; Luke 5.1–11; John 21; Acts 2–3; 10–11.18; Galatians 2–3.

Bibliography

Raymond E. Brown, Karl P. Donfield, John Reumann (eds), *Peter in the New Testament*, Chapman 1973; Oscar Cullmann, *Peter: Disciple, Apostle, Martyr*, SCM Press, 2nd edition 1962; J. K. Elliott, 'Κηφᾶς: Σίμων Πέτρος: ὁ Πέτρος: An Examination of New Testament Usage', *Novum Testamentum* XIX, 1972, pp. 241–56.

8 Who was St Paul?

The New Testament contains thirteen letters in Paul's name. These are among the earliest Christian documents to have survived, and are therefore of especial importance in an investigation of the earliest days of the church. In addition Paul is the only writer in the New Testament who claims to have witnessed a resurrection appearance, and for this reason many consider his words to be of particular significance.

Of the thirteen letters, most scholars argue that the Pastoral Epistles (I and II Timothy and Titus), Colossians and Ephesians although written in Paul's name were not in fact by the same author as the rest of the Pauline corpus. The language, style, historical context and the theology of these letters are so different from the authentic Pauline letters (Romans, I and II Corinthians, Galatians, Philippians, I and II Thessalonians and Philemon) that it is unlikely that they came from his pen. We have already seen in the previous chapter that letters were written in the name of the leader of the disciples (I and II Peter) and in the name of the leader of Jesus' family (James). It is therefore not surprising that those writing within the tradition and from the viewpoint of Paul wrote letters in his name too. Pseudonymous writings were conventional in the first century and it is not to be thought that any dishonest motive or piracy are implied by its use. To dedicate a work to the leader of one's school of thought by presenting it in his name was an act of homage and honour.

Of the undisputed Pauline letters the majority were written to churches founded by Paul. These include the epistles to Corinth, Galatia, Philippi and Thessalonica. No doubt other letters were written by Paul to other churches: even in the extant correspondence Paul refers to letters that have not survived. From those that have been preserved we gain a varied picture of church life in the earliest days of the separate Christian communities. Most of Paul's letters deal with the immediate problems and questions raised by members of these early churches. For the most part therefore the epistles are spontaneous reactions by Paul either replying to these questions or dealing with issues that have cropped up where he needs to state an opinion. Topics covered in this way range from the eating of food offered to idols, the apparent delay in the second coming, marriage with unbelievers and the presence of false teachers. Any theological teaching that appears is usually within the context of dealing with a current problem such as these.

The letter which is an exception is the one Paul wrote to the Christians in Rome. In this epistle Paul is writing with some circumspection and at some length to a Christian community that he did not found. Here he gives a fuller and more developed exposition of his theology. Instead of dealing with current issues this writing is more of a theological treatise. We shall investigate below possible reasons why Paul felt obliged to set out his theological views to the church at the centre of the Empire. The teaching given in the letter to the Romans is probably to be compared with that given orally to the churches Paul himself had established. It is certainly likely that what Paul wrote to Rome was not being newly thought out. Many well polished phrases and metaphors, reflex-action proof texts and a certain degree of coherence and completeness about many of the arguments presented in the letter suggest that much of it, however physically protracted the actual writing process, contains material that was frequently on Paul's lips. One feels that Paul in this letter is using arguments regularly to be found in his earlier teaching and preaching.

Nevertheless despite the detailed theological exposé in Romans and the more pragmatic teaching in the other epistles there is much in all the letters about Paul's missionary activities which is of value for an historical investigation into the origins of Christianity. It must however be remembered that Paul did not set out to give detailed historical notes. For the most part his letters were not intended to be preserved. Still less did he intend to include rich biographical detail.

The churches founded by him would know his personal history, and even in writing to Rome Paul assumes his readers have heard of him. History and biographical information are however present to some extent in all the epistles and it is to them we turn as primary documents for details about Paul's life and work.

The Acts of the Apostles almost makes Paul its hero, but as we saw in Chapter 6 this work is of limited historical value. In its attempt to eliminate the major differences between Paul and Peter, or rather between the pro-gentile and pro-Jewish branches of the church, and in its attempts to portray the gradual progression of Christianity from Jerusalem to Rome the author has often sacrificed or ignored historical fact and instead has made use of legendary material. That is not to say that Acts is worthless as an historical document. In many places Acts confirms what Paul writes. But on other occasions Paul's evidence is at variance with Acts. The rule of thumb to be adopted is that where such conflict occurs, Paul's account is more likely to represent the truth, other things being equal. Paul's writing was usually concerned with current matters but where he tells of past events in his life he stands close to them. Acts on the other hand although incorporating primitive material especially in the earlier chapters was written about forty to fifty years after the events Paul speaks of. Nowhere does Acts refer to or show any knowledge of Paul's letters. Acts is an independent source betraying the theological presuppositions of the author.

The authentic Pauline letters are usually dated from about 51–57 during which time Paul seems to have spent eighteen months in Corinth, and over two years in Ephesus. If the reference in Acts to Paul's being in court in Corinth during the time Gallio was proconsul of Achaia (Acts 18.12) is accurate this enables Paul's work at this time to be dated about the years 51–52. This together with other internally ascertainable clues enables scholars to piece together the rough time scale of Paul's operations and writings. I Thessalonians is usually dated as the earliest letter we possess although some scholars put Galatians first. The destination of the Galatian letter is a crux of New Testament scholarship: if Paul were writing to the churches in South Galatia the date could be as early as 51 soon after the Council of Jerusalem at the beginning of the second missionary journey, if Paul were writing to the churches in North Galatia it cannot be as early: Paul founded the churches in the North only on his second missionary journey. The letters to Corinth and Philippi and the personal letter to Philemon were probably composed about 55–56. The last letter written is Romans possibly in 57 and reveals plans by Paul to visit Rome en route for Spain, after having called in at Jerusalem with the collection of money made among Christians in Greece for the poor in Jerusalem. As events turn out, at least according to Acts, Paul does visit Rome after his visit to Jerusalem but not as a free agent: he is arrested in Jerusalem and taken first to Caesarea and then by sea to Rome.

By analysing the personal details in the authentic Pauline letters and by comparing these with Acts a reasonably coherent picture of Paul emerges. Where discrepancies occur between Paul and Acts we shall accept the historicity of the former. Conservatives and literalists determined at all costs to avoid any suggestion of discrepancies in holy writ or of historical inaccuracy try to explain away these difficulties and to reconcile Paul and Acts, but such attempts are usually strained and involve much special pleading.

I

Acts has Paul say in 22.3 that he was a native of Tarsus in Cilicia, in present-day Turkey. As there is no obvious theological reason why that is important to Acts we may assert the historicity of this statement. Acts also states (7.58; 8.1,3; 9.1,8) that Paul's original name was Saul. Here we may suspect inaccuracy. Acts may well be attempting by means of this easy change of name to bring Paul into line with the famous Old Testament king who like Paul was also a Benjamite. Acts has as one of its main themes that of Paul the loyal Jew and therefore would find such a comparison significant. In his letters Paul never calls himself Saul.

Paul's Jewish background is however unquestionable. He refers to it on numerous occasions. From II Cor. 11.22; Rom. 11.1; Phil. 3.5 we learn he is Israelite of the tribe of Benjamin and a Pharisee. Paul's motive in emphasizing this aspect of his life is first in order to point to the similarity between himself and the Jerusalem church apostles, and secondly to show the contrast between his own pre-conversion state and his Christian life.

His upbringing in Tarsus placed him in the liberal and proselytizing Judaism of the diaspora. This made him different from the Jerusalem based church leaders whose lives seem to have centred on the temple and who would have been influenced by its cultus, priesthood and sacrifices. There is no reference in Paul's own letters to any contact with Jerusalem before his conversion to Christianity. His tutelage under Gamaliel in Jerusalem referred to in Acts 22.3 is not substantiated in his letters and may be due to Luke's continuing efforts in Acts to give Paul roots in Jerusalem.

Acts and Paul agree in having Paul a persecutor of the early church. As a loyal Pharisee Paul would have found much that was offensive to him in the Christian proclamation. Many of the hostile references to Pharisees in the gospels reflect the antagonism between Christians and Pharisees in the nascent church. Matthew 23 for example is given over almost completely to denunciation of Pharisees. After his conversion Paul ceased persecuting the church and instead joined it as one of its most active workers. Acts has him persecute Christians in both Damascus and Jerusalem but probably Damascus was Paul's sphere of influence.

Jesus' movement began in the Galilee but after his death was based in Judaea. After the first Easter some of Jesus' former companions and his family seem to have put down roots in Jerusalem. Acts does not give details of this changed base for operations, but it does seem that Christianity soon spread from there but with some problems. Despite its general tendency to portray a harmonious church Acts (6.1–6) shows that early in its existence a split developed between the diaspora Jewish Christians and the Jerusalem church. Acts tells how the Hellenists in the church broke with the Hebrews. Stephen and the other leaders of the Hellenists were allegedly elected by the Hebrews. All of these so-called Hellenistic deacons significantly have Greek names (Acts 6.5). We may suspect here that by referring to an election Acts is trying to paper over the cracks. The differences though seem to have been both real and deep. The Hellenists must have been among the first converts by the Jerusalem church but like Paul later seem to have been less circumspect in dealing with that church's leaders or with the Jews. The split resulted not only in the martyrdom of Stephen whose trial and death have been written up by Luke in Acts on the model of Jesus' trials and death, but also in the dispersion of the Hellenized Christians to Phoenicia, Cyprus and

Antioch (Acts 11.19). This left the Jerusalem church in the hands of the original apostles who seem to have developed and maintained a *modus vivendi* with the Jewish authorities (Acts 8.1).

Acts 8 preserves the tradition that those who had been persecuted by the Jerusalem church preached elsewhere. Philip is said to have worked in Samaria. It is interesting to note that after he had founded a (Hellenized) Christian community there the Jerusalem church authorities soon dispatched two of its leaders (Peter and John) to validate the orthodoxy of the teaching (Acts 8.14) in the same way as later Pauline churches were contacted and indoctrinated by the Jerusalem church.

Damascus seems to have been another centre of Hellenized Christianity, and is where Paul first encountered the church. Acts 9.2 shows that he persecuted the Damascus church, and Acts 9.19,22 shows he first preached Christianity there. In the meantime his conversion seems to have occurred in the area of Damascus. Acts, on three occasions (9.1f.; 22.3f. and 26.9f.), tells of his conversion. If the auditory and visionary experience described there is what Paul has in mind at I Cor. 15.8 when he says Christ appeared to him then Luke's portrayal of Paul's resurrection experience in Acts was very different from the stories of the appearances of the risen Christ in the Easter narratives in his gospel. Paul's own description of his conversion is less dramatic and merely includes the statement that he is to be counted among those who were granted a resurrection appearance. In II. Cor. 12.2 he speaks of a Christian man, presumably himself, who was 'caught up into paradise' – again no details are given but it is presumed that this too refers to Paul's conversion. The actual conversion of Paul to Christianity may well have taken place less dramatically over a long period of contemplation in Damascus. Whatever happened to Paul, the conversion was however a real one and lasted the rest of his life. The tradition that Paul the Christian lived in Damascus is found not only in Acts 9.18, 22.10f. but in the letters. According to Gal. 1.15–17 it was to Damascus that Paul returned after a post-conversion sojourn in Arabia.

Where Acts is at variance with the letters is in stating that soon after his conversion Paul was introduced to the church in Jerusalem where he then stayed. We again note that this is another instance of Luke's basing Paul in Jerusalem. The letters, in particular Galatians, emphasize Paul's independence of Jerusalem. Galatians 1.17 denies any journey to Jerusalem at this stage. Paul states it was only after three years that he visited Jerusalem and then saw Peter (called as so often by Paul 'Kephas' to emphasize his Jewishness) and James whose name is added as an afterthought. After this visit Gal. 1.21–23 states that he preached in Syria and Cilicia without any contact with Jerusalem. Acts tells us nothing of this. We do not learn either there or in the letters of Paul's work or success in Arabia, Syria or Cilicia. Paul claims in Gal. 1.24 that the Jerusalem church leadership was appreciative of the reports reaching them that the former persecutor of the church was now an evangelist. They seem not to have interfered with Paul, possibly because they were unaware of the content of his preaching; indeed he makes plain that this work was unknown to those in Judaea (Gal. 1.22). It was only later when Paul began preaching in Cyprus and Asia Minor that the Jerusalem church took action to curb Paul's activities. In the earliest days after his conversion Paul seems to have been left undisturbed. The unimportance of Paul's work at this stage in his Christian career is possibly why Acts is silent here.

The reason why Paul shifted his attention to the mediterranean may well have been due to his apparent lack of success in those areas to the north and east of Palestine, but it also seems to have been due to a change of base from Damascus to Antioch.

Barnabas seems to have been the leader of the breakaway Hellenized church in Antioch (Acts 11.20–24) and it appears that he was responsible for introducing Paul to that important city. Acts, which ignores Paul's feeble efforts at evangelizing in Cilicia and Syria, has Paul brought to Antioch from Tarsus (Acts 11.25–26) – Paul himself does not refer to this.

The name 'Christians' seems to have developed first in Antioch according to Acts 11.26. This breakaway and international church (Acts 13.1) attracted this name for its adherents because of their identifiable difference from both their Jewish and pagan neighbours. It is significant that Antiochene Christianity with its apparent distinctiveness became Paul's new base.

In the period between the first visit to Jerusalem referred to in Gal. 1.18 and the second in Gal. 2.1 Paul seems to have been influenced by Barnabas. Acts 11.26 says that Paul and Barnabas worked together in Antioch for a long period. During this time Acts says Paul and Barnabas visited the Jerusalem church with relief for Christians suffering there from a famine which occurred during Claudius' reign. Such contacts with the Jerusalem church occur in Paul's later work when he encourages churches in Greece to contribute to the mother church, but this visit in Acts 11.27–30 is unlikely to be historical. Galatians is firm about the number of contacts Paul had with Jerusalem and this famine relief visit cannot easily be accommodated in his timetable. We may dismiss this visit in Acts as yet another attempt to link Paul with Jerusalem.

It is with Barnabas that Acts says Paul undertook a missionary journey from Antioch to Cyprus and the southern parts of Asia Minor. This journey is not referred to in Paul's letters, but in essence is likely to be historical. If Galatians is addressed to churches in South Galatia these churches would have been founded on that journey. Acts 13–14 contains much legendary material about these journeys. Much of the material seems to have been modelled on equally legendary stories concerning Peter which occur earlier in Acts. The incidents recorded take place in Salamis, Paphos, Perga, Pisidian Antioch, Iconium, Lystra and Derbe. After this journey Acts has Paul and Barnabas appear in Jerusalem because certain persons from Judaea were objecting to Paul's and Barnabas' practice of allowing converts to Christianity to bypass Judaism (Acts 15.1–2). Scholars have debated if this visit is the second of the two visits to Jerusalem which Paul mentions in Gal. 2.1. On balance it is likely that Gal. 2 and Acts 15 tell of the same conference, albeit from differing ideological standpoints. The congress was called to question Paul and Barnabas about their preaching. Although Galatians does not specify the motive for this it looks as if it was due to Paul's increasingly successful evangelizing. His work on the so-called first missionary journey, that is on the first missionary journey recounted by Acts, could well have brought the Jerusalem authorities' attention to Paul's theology.

During this summit meeting held in the late forties Paul shows in Gal. 2 that he asserted with vehemence his independence of the so-called pillars of the Jerusalem church. His claim is that far from being *summoned* to Jerusalem he went up by divine command. The only bridle which Paul claims was imposed on his evangelistic activity was that he should maintain contact with the mother church in Jerusalem by providing money for their poorer members. Even this obligation is, according to Paul, something he wished to do anyway! He implies that the Council accepted that he and Barnabas were to continue to evangelize the gentiles. The account of this Council in Acts on the other hand has Paul bridled with further regulations obliging him to impose on his converts certain Jewish ritualistic requirements. If such a decree were issued Paul does not refer to it. In his discussions on food regulations in I Corinthians and Romans he betrays no knowledge of any such regulations. One particularly significant detail in the account in Acts is that the regulations were set out in a letter and distributed to Antioch, Syria and Cilicia (Acts 15.23f.) in other words to places where Paul had worked. This might suggest that once Paul's work did reach the Jerusalem church leaders they attempted to establish their authority in places Paul had visited. This detail in Acts could have reached Luke from a tradition known in these churches that James tried to impose Jewish regulations on them. However, the account of the Council in Acts is itself unlikely to be historical. The regulations as accepted by Paul attempt to blur the differences between the two branches of the church and fit in with the distinctive theological pattern imposed by the author of Acts on his material.

That is not to say that Paul's account of these events in Gal. 2 is itself entirely accurate. The conclusion of the Council meeting given by him is idealistic. In implying that his freedom to preach to gentiles was ratified at the highest level by James, Kephas and John he doubtless tried to sound impressive when writing to the churches in Galatia who were in need of such assertiveness if they were to remain unshaken in their confidence in Pauline Christianity. It is unlikely that the pillars of the Jerusalem establishment would have agreed to Paul's untrammelled access to a gentile constituency. Had the right hand of friendship been proferred to Paul (Gal. 2.9) it is improbable that Paul would have encountered so much opposition from the pro-Jewish Christians later. It was because of such trouble in Galatia that this letter had to be written and as we shall see later other letters refer to similar opposition.

Although Paul and Barnabas worked together in and from Antioch, and appeared as partners at the apostolic Council in Jerusalem the partnership did not survive. Soon after the conference Gal. 2.11–14 shows that Paul was branding not only Kephas but Barnabas as a hypocrite. The reason for this outburst on Paul's part seems to have been that the Jerusalem church leaders, despite the alleged treaty of friendship just described, tried to impose Jewish dietary regulations on the Christians in Antioch – Barnabas complied and thus betrayed his principles. Although Paul had found Antioch a convenient base and Barnabas a congenial partner during some of the fourteen years between the two visits to Jerusalem he refers to in Galatians, Barnabas' outlook differed from Paul's. Even Acts refers to the split between the two men (Acts 15.39). Barnabas seems to have been closer to Kephas than to Paul and unlike Paul was unwilling to make a complete break with Judaism. John Mark who accompanied Paul and Barnabas on the first missionary journey deserted them in Perga (Acts 13.13) for reasons unspecified. Perhaps he like Barnabas soon afterwards found Paul's intransigence unbearable. After the break with Paul, Barnabas and John Mark set out on their own evangelizing mission to Cyprus (Acts 15.39). Antiochene Christianity therefore seems to have stood midway between the Jerusalem church and Paul. Some scholars argue that the gospels of Matthew and possibly Luke originated in Antioch and reflect that theological position. Thus within only a few years of the church's existence schism had occurred.

After the break with Barnabas, Paul did not use Antioch as a base. With other companions he roamed the mediterranean maintaining reluctant but loose contact with Jerusalem. The majority of Paul's letters were composed at different points on these journeys as he kept in touch with the churches he founded. The opening and concluding greetings to his letters, and Rom. 16 in particular show that Paul quickly gathered around him a band of loyal friends, the majority of whom bore Greek names and lived outside Palestine.

The first of the journeys Paul made after the Council is told in characteristic style in Acts 16.1–18.22. Here Paul with Silas and subsequently Timothy revisited Derbe, Lystra and Iconium before going to Troas, Macedonia and Greece. Churches were founded in Philippi, Thessalonica and Corinth (and in Galatia if Galatians was written to the northern province of Galatia). The journey seems to have taken about five years of which eighteen months were spent in Corinth. As in its accounts of the first missionary journey Acts includes many legendary elements and inserts inspiring speeches into Paul's mouth. The story of the jail break in Philippi seems to have been modelled on the earlier story of Peter's escape from prison. After the visit to Philippi Paul and his companions moved to Thessalonica and had to escape from that city to Beroea because of a riot. This detail is corroborated in Paul's letter to the church in Thessalonica sent shortly after his escape (I Thess. 2.2). After further trouble in Beroea Acts has Paul make an impressive speech in Athens which had little success. Then he moved on to Corinth where he stayed and worked at his trade as tentmaker. Here he established a successful church with which he maintained contact. The end of this second missionary journey is recorded with brevity by Acts. Acts 18.18 tells how he went to Ephesus and Caesarea, then returned to his old haunts in Antioch. Nothing is told of this visit, but it is significant that he avoids a journey to Jerusalem and sets off again on another journey, the third in Acts.

On this journey Paul revisited North Galatia and returned to Ephesus this time to stay for over two years, during which he seems to have spent a period in jail. Acts knows nothing of this but many scholars are convinced that the letters to Philippi and to Philemon which suggest Paul is in captivity are to be dated from this time rather than from Rome later. Acts 19 includes legends about Paul in Ephesus before relating how he set out for Macedonia and Greece. According to Acts 20.3 a plot on his life made Paul leave Greece for Jerusalem. It is on this third missionary journey that most of Paul's letters were written. In Romans 15.28 Paul expresses his desire to visit Rome: in the Acts account of this journey this intention is also attributed to Paul (Acts 19.21).

One of the major areas of agreement between Paul's letters and Acts is that in both sources we hear of regular opposition to Paul. He is followed by troublemakers throughout his missionary work. In Acts, trouble in Lystra (Acts 14.19–20) is occasioned by Jews coming from Antioch and Iconium and he is stoned; at Philippi he is jailed; in Thessalonica the mob is incited by the Jews out of jealousy of Paul (17.5); in Beroea the same people dog him (17.13); in Corinth he is put in court (18.12); in Ephesus there is a riot (19.28–29). (I Cor. 16.9 and II Cor. 1.8–10 speak of opposition in Ephesus which made him despair of life.) Opposition to the Christian movement in Acts comes, as it does in Luke's gospel, from the Jews. In the final chapters in Acts the Jews of Jerusalem and Caesarea are hostile to Paul (Acts 21.27–29; 22.22f.; 23.12; 25.7). By contrast Paul like his Lord before him finds that the gentiles treat him well – he is befriended by the commandant of the cohort (21.37f., 23.19–35), then the procurator Felix and later Festus behave in a somewhat similar way to Pilate (24.26 and 25.9). Also, like Jesus in Luke's gospel, Paul has to appear on trial not only before a governor but a king (cf. Acts 4.26): in Paul's case the king is Agrippa and he is convinced of Paul's innocence (Acts 26).

Paul's own letters stress the opposition he encountered, but whereas Acts blames the Jews Paul points to the Jewish Christians as his opponents. Let us survey the references to hostility as they occur in the letters. We have already had occasion to examine the vehement hostility between Paul and the Jerusalem church leaders revealed in Gal. 1–2. The opponents are trying to pervert Paul's original message to the Galatians (Gal. 1.6). He claims that unnamed persons are envious of his converts (Gal. 4.17). It is clear from Gal. 5.2 that the perversion of Paul's message is the insistence that Galatian converts accept circumcision. In particular Paul seems to have one individual opponent in mind (Gal. 5.7–8) and he states that this man's message is not divinely inspired. Circumcision to Paul is symbolic of the imposition of Judaism with its outmoded legalism. To him circumcision is a mutilation. In Gal. 6.12–13 he argues that those who insist on circumcision for converts do so only to gain power for themselves by wresting from him the credit for winning for the Christian cause converts in his own way. 'Uncircumcision' becomes the watchword of his party just as 'circumcision' is the keynote of the Jerusalem church.

In I Thessalonians opposition is not a dominant theme but even here Paul says that his several attempts at revisiting the church were thwarted in Thessalonica by 'Satan' (I Thess. 2.18). Possibly a human agent is in mind because in 3.5 he acknowledges his anxiety about the Thessalonians' steadfastness to their original faith as he fears a tempter might have been influencing them. There is academic dispute about the authenticity of II Thessalonians but on balance this epistle seems to be Pauline. In this letter Paul warns the church not to allow anyone to deceive them (II Thess. 2.3) and warns the

Christians there not to deviate from the traditions he taught (II Thess. 2.6, 15). Paul even suggests that the opposing views have been expressed in a pseudonymous letter (II Thess. 2.2).

Further opposition to Paul's teaching is found in Philippi. In Phil. 1.15–18 Paul contrasts the methods by which Christianity is proclaimed: there are those who proclaim it in goodwill and are pro-Pauline, and there are those who are jealous and quarrelsome and who aim at making trouble for Paul. In Phil. 3.2–3 he identifies the latter as those who insist on circumcision – to Paul such people are dogs practising evil.

It is in the longer Corinthian correspondence that rival groups are spoken of with great detail. There seems to have been a schism in that church between those who follow certain factions. Three of the groups are the Kephas party, the Paul party and the Apollos party. (I Cor. 1.12; 3.4–5, 22). As the founder of the church in Corinth Paul jealously guards his patch and begrudges these parvenus any rights there. He warns the church that his foundation teaching must not be altered (I Cor. 3.11) and sends Timothy to remind the church of his teaching (I Cor. 4.17). It appears that, among others, Kephas travelled to Corinth and persuaded at least a section of the church there to reject Paul's distinctive teaching. Kephas' credentials and behaviour met with particular approval with the church: these were to Paul's detriment (I Cor. 9.1–5). The Corinthians seem to have accepted Kephas as a better apostle. Even in the matter of sending the gift of money to Jerusalem Paul's honesty was questioned. In I Cor. 16.3 he makes elaborate plans whereby the cash will be dispatched with people of their own choosing who are to be furnished with a letter of introduction by Paul. Such a level of mistrust had been fostered between Paul and this church that in II Cor. 8.20 Paul says he does not wish to allow himself to be criticized for the way he handled the cash. The angry and emotional letter which is known as II Corinthians bristles with rage against those who do not acknowledge his apostleship. Just as the church distrusted Paul's honesty with money so too this church doubted the honesty of his intentions when he made excuses about not visiting Corinth (II Cor. 1.15–18). This attitude hardly suggests the warm father-child relationship Paul himself fondly hopes for in Corinth. Possibly the influence of those who arrived in Corinth after Paul had established the church made his converts reassess their attitude towards their founder. II Corinthians 3.1 speaks of 'some people' who having been introduced to the Corinthian church then questioned Paul's credentials. In II Cor. 10.7–10 he defends the validity of his Christian teaching by saying it is as sincere as 'a certain other man's' and he suggests his personal prestige has recently been disparaged by this man. The painful visit referred to in II Cor. 2.1 and the sorrowful letter of II Cor. 2.4 were apparently emotional responses by Paul to the abuse he claims was levelled against him in his absence. He felt his apostleship had been denigrated. The identity of the mysterious 'someone' who figures in many of these tirades may be identified as one of the Jerusalem church leaders. In II Cor. 11.4–6 the following words occur: 'For if *someone* comes who proclaims another Jesus not the Jesus whom we proclaimed or if you receive a spirit different from the spirit you received or a gospel different from the gospel you have already accepted you submit to it readily enough. I am not in the least inferior to those superlative apostles. Even if I am unskilled in speaking I am not in knowledge; at all times we have made known to you the full truth.' The phrase 'superlative apostles' here recalls for us the pillars of the church who are reputed to be something in Gal. 2. II Corinthians 12.11–12 re-enforces this comparison and deals with the problem Paul has in asserting his apostleship: 'In no respect did I fall short of these superlative apostles even if I am a nobody'. (Cf. also II Cor. 11.12–15: 'I shall go on doing as I am doing now to cut the ground under those who would seize any chance to put their vaunted apostleship on the same level as ours. Such men are false apostles and deceitful workmen masquerading as apostles of Christ. There is nothing surprising about that: Satan himself masquerades as an angel of light. It is therefore a simple thing for his agents to masquerade as angels of good. But they will meet the end their deeds deserve.') Strong language indeed! None of the pro-Jewish Jerusalem church leaders is said by Paul to be more of a Hebrew, an Israelite or a descendant of Abraham than Paul himself (II Cor. 11.22f.). Thus we are able to identify the cause of opposition to Paul as Jewish Christians who are called 'superlative apostles' and whose watchword is circumcision.

It might be thought that the epistle to the Romans would be free of this pervading controversy. The umbilical cord that attached Paul to Corinth is not present in the letter written to strangers but his attitude to the Judaizers here is similar to that in the other letters.

The simmering hostility is present and Paul characteristically speaks out even though he is conscious he is building on another man's foundations – a practice condemned in Corinth and also in Rom. 15.20 itself. Circumcision and the law were such vital issues in the controversies Paul was involved in with Jerusalem that he states his views on these issues not only in Galatians and Philippians but also in depth in Romans. Romans is a detailed expression of Paul's views on these matters. Having set out his gospel in this letter Paul's old antagonism to his opponents breaks out in Rom. 15.22. It seems from this verse that as in Thessalonica Paul was 'prevented' from visiting the church. He then asks the Romans to pray for him in coping with the 'unbelievers' in Judaea. He is about to visit Jerusalem and doubts his success. Romans 16.17–20 warns the readers to avoid those who 'stir up quarrels' and 'lead people astray' by preaching a new doctrine. This chapter was probably not originally part of the letter to Rome but shows that the theme of opposition was a regular preoccupation. If this chapter was sent to Ephesus, as some scholars argue, then the reference to the new doctrine would suggest a gospel in opposition to Paul's as in Gal. 1.6.

Even though it is very unlikely that Colossians and Ephesians were written by Paul it is significant to note that the theme of circumcision continues to be dominant as a dividing line between the pro-Pauline church which was responsible for perpetuating Paul's teaching in these letters, and the pro-Jewish Christians (Col. 2.11; 3.11; Eph. 2.11–12). Colossians 2.16 shows that a major preoccupation in this church was the imposition of sabbath and dietary regulations on the church by outsiders. As in Rom. 14 and I Cor. 8 and 10 food regulations were another dividing line between the two branches of the church. As we saw in chapter 3 these preoccupations played their part in the formation of the gospel material.

Paul's final years are obscure. We have had cause to be suspicious of Acts especially in those narratives telling of Paul's exploits. Similarly the speeches attributed to him in Acts are Lukan compositions and in no way related to the real Paul of the letters. Thus it is unlikely that the story of Paul's arrest, trial and imprisonment in Jerusalem and Caesarea is authentic. As we have seen, the confrontations with the gentile commandant, and with Felix, Festus and Agrippa are modelled on Jesus' arrest and trials. Similarly the long sea voyage to Rome is unlikely to be historic. In the closing chapters Paul the prisoner turns into Paul the evangelist. He performs miracles and is entertained in Malta; he stays a week with Christians in Puteoli; and he is met as a distinguished visitor at the Forum of Appius and Three Taverns on the Appian Way and brought triumphantly to Rome. Even in Rome Paul is given his own house with free access to Jews who are unsullied by Judaea (Acts 28.21). Paul preaches to them, and lives at his own expense. Acts says this state of affairs lasted two years. Some scholars argue that a further period of missionary activity followed release from this house arrest, but this cannot be proved. Others argue that Paul was killed in Rome, but that Luke deemed it unedifying to end Acts with its hero's martyrdom. All that can be said with certainty is that the purpose of Acts to have Paul arrive in Rome is fulfilled.

So far as the likeliest historical reconstruction of events is concerned all that is known from the epistles is that Paul is on the way to Jerusalem with money collected among the churches. He had not visited Jerusalem since the apostolic Council and is apprehensive about the visit. The continuing opposition most of which seems to have originated in Jerusalem did not augur well for his reception. No further authentic letters came from his pen after his letter to Rome. If Paul was arrested in Jerusalem and sent to Rome for trial it is unlikely to have been as Acts tells. We have only church tradition that both Peter and Paul died as martyrs in Rome: the New Testament does not tell us. Paul's career after writing Romans must remain a mystery.

II

Having reviewed Paul's career it is significant to recall that a common theme running through his life and missionary work as it is recorded in Acts and in his own letters is that of opposition. The reasons for such hostility to him are threefold: first his Christian message was theologically provocative; secondly his background made the earliest Christians view him with suspicion; thirdly his assumption of apostleship was resented. Let us examine each of these.

Paul's letters suggest that the majority of Christians in his day were non-Jewish. Paul's conspicuous success in recruiting gentiles to Christianity is the *raison d'être* of his ministry – he speaks of himself as the apostle to the gentiles on several occasions (Rom. 15.16; Gal. 1.16; 2.9; I Thess. 2.16). His success was the cause as well as the result of his theological beliefs. As a Jew of the diaspora Paul, unlike the Jerusalem church leaders, had close connections with the proselytizing movement in the first century. He had also been more familiar with the Godfearers on the fringes of the synagogue movement. The respect with which Jews were regarded in most of the Empire made it a religious movement favoured by many non-Jews. For Paul to emphasize his Jewish background was to set himself up as a man to be respected. His earliest missionary work in Syria and Cilicia seem not to have borne fruit, yet when he moved out of Palestine and Syria to Cyprus, Asia Minor and Greece more and more adherents to his Christian message came from outside Judaism. Paul probably began his preaching at each new location in the synagogue. Although it would suit the theology of Acts to emphasize Paul's visiting the synagogues first in each new town this course of action is nevertheless likely to be historical. Whether it was Paul's original intention to reach out to non-Jews or not is difficult to judge, but given his success with the gentiles he rethought and presented his theology in the light of his experiences. Certainly Paul had to reassess his ideas about God's scheme of salvation for all mankind. The distinctiveness of the Jews, their covenants, traditions and the Mosaic law were not things which a man of Paul's background and learning could easily reject as worthless.

The conflict between his background and his Christian mission is vividly described in his letters. The realization that circumcision and the law were irrelevant because they had been superseded by belief in the risen Christ is a constant theme in his writings. The belief that the age-old promises to Abraham were intended for gentiles is the guiding light of Paul's missionary activity. His arguments that Judaism's unique privileges were now obsolete are doubtless reasons why he fell foul of the pro-Jewish leaders of the Jerusalem church. To believe as he did that Christianity was universal gave his preaching worldwide appeal. The epistle to the Romans shows how Paul came to this belief albeit with much heartsearching.

Paul's constant theme is that man is living in a new age of the spirit which has been effected by Christ's resurrection. His confident hope is that those who have been mystically united with Christ by having been baptized will share with Christ in a resurrection like his. The cycle of sin and death initiated by the fall and reinforced by the Mosaic law had been broken. For Paul Christ is the firstfruits of those raised from the dead, and that was revolutionary. Judaism contained the belief that at some future period God would stretch out his hand into She'ol and awaken the sleeping spirits. But this belief was not dominant. For Paul though this event had already happened in the resurrection of Christ. The slender suggestion that there would be a general resurrection of the dead found occasionally in the Old Testament became for Paul a matter of confident hope. It was this confidence which enervated his teaching. His ethical precepts took on a new significance. Paul speaks of man sinning against a body destined for immortality. The power – if not the immediate effects – of sin, namely death, had been broken. The cosmic and timeless significance of Christ's historic death is one of the most difficult concepts in Christian theology but was of over-riding significance for Paul who believed that the effects of the fall had been reversed: Christ was the new Adam.

This resumé of Paul's theology serves only to emphasize that his teaching was based on a belief in the fact that the exclusiveness claimed by Jews was irreconcilable with belief in Christ. But it is this theology which brought him into conflict with the Jerusalem church.

It is interesting to speculate about the teaching given by Paul to churches other than the church in Rome. Paul obviously had to present as clearly as possible his distinctive gospel to Rome because he felt the Christians there had been prejudiced against his views by its founder (Peter?). One assumes that a message similar to that written to Rome was given orally by Paul to the churches he himself founded. Much of the argumentation in Paul's writing – and presumably in his preaching too, although he claims no skill in oratory, is Rabbinic in style and presupposes knowledge of Jewish history and tradition. Certainly many arguments are based on reinterpretations of Old Testament passages. This does not imply that even a majority of his readers were Jewish. If the original members of the earliest church communities were from the fringes of the synagogue movement then such presuppositions would be familiar to them. One of the appeals of Paul's message to these Godfearers was that they were told that as Christians they inherited the benefits previously jealously reserved for Jews. A non-Jewish adherent of the synagogue movement would be a second class member: as a Christian he was told by Paul that although originally a part of a wild olive tree he was now grafted on to the cultivated olive tree of Judaism (Rom. 11. 13–18). To Paul the true fulfilment of Judaism was Christianity – the historical Judaism was the trunk of the tree but gentiles could be grafted in and share its benefits. This belief, anathema though it was to the majority of Jews, was largely responsible for Paul's maintaining contact with the Jerusalem church which he saw as a link with Judaism, and the earthly Jesus.

The second reason for Paul's attracting opposition is to be found in his background. The change from being a persecutor of the church to being a fervent Christian was not forgotten. On several occasions Paul refers to his background only to demonstrate that his conversion to Christianity had been a complete *volte-face*. Philippians 3.1–11; Gal. 1.13; II Cor. 12 refer to the contrast between his pre-Christian and present life. Others no doubt could not forget Paul's earlier antagonism to the church and thus were wary of his credentials.

The third reason why Paul was looked at with suspicion is that unlike the Jerusalem church leaders it is improbable that he knew the earthly Jesus. The Jesus of the ministry was of little importance to Paul: he hardly refers in his letters to the acts and sayings of Jesus. Possibly he had been told something about Jesus when he visited Peter (Gal. 1.18) but the meaning of the verb in that verse is not clear. For Paul only the changed relationship between man and God wrought by the death and resurrection are significant. Jesus' life is but a prelude to that allegedly salvific act. Echoes of Jesus' teaching some of which found their way into the gospels as sayings of Jesus may be located in Paul's writings but they do not dominate his theology.

The earliest Christians were however being confronted not only by Paul but also by those who had known Jesus in his lifetime and it is apparent that the appeal such people had in the church made Paul look less significant. His inferiority complex makes him emphasize on several occasions his equality with the Jerusalem church leaders. Paul cannot appeal to personal knowledge of Jesus in his lifetime.

Instead he stresses his contact with the risen Lord. In the list of resurrection appearances in I Cor. 15 he claims to have been privy to a Christophany just as Peter and James had. Most of the letters state that his missionary work was activated by a personal commission by God. Apostleship even in Acts is denied to Paul – there the original disciples of Jesus are the apostles. But Paul assumes this title for himself and in many of his letters introduces himself in the address as Paul an apostle due to God's call. Denial by others of his right to use this title encouraged Paul's self-conscious parading of his commission. Paul believed he was a real apostle.

Despite the opposition aroused, Paul's theological contribution to Christianity is enormous but his main work was in bringing what originally began as a messianic and renovating movement within Judaism to a worldwide audience. His message of universal salvation was a success even in his own lifetime. However much he exaggerates in II Cor. 11.21–27 the punishments he underwent in his travels, it is clear he did not spare himself. The mysterious 'thorn in the flesh' which cannot easily be diagnosed implies he was not in good health. Mentally too he was in torment. The conflicts within himself as he tried to reconcile his new Christian life with his former Jewish upbringing give his writing a poignant and dramatic impact. Yet it is due to this restlessness that many churches were founded, some of which survived beyond Paul's own day.

The geographical spread of Christianity owes much to his efforts, but Paul cannot be credited with all such evangelization. Because of the influence of Acts we tend to think that only Paul and his companions were instrumental in spreading Christianity beyond Palestine. As we have already seen the church in Rome was not founded by him. This church was flourishing and influential within twenty years of Jesus' death. A church was also founded in Colossae to which a pseudonymous letter of Paul's was addressed. That letter also knows of churches in Laodicea and Hierapolis (Col. 4.13) which are non-Pauline in origin. I Corinthians 9.5 speaks of the apostles, Kephas and Jesus' family travelling around evangelizing – and thwarting Paul – in among other places Corinth itself. We also know from church history that Christianity reached Egypt early. Again Paul is unlikely to have travelled there: the New Testament in fact knows of no missionary activity south of Palestine, although Acts

2.10 speaks of Egyptian Christians at Pentecost. There was therefore much missionary activity within twenty years of Jesus' death: Paul successful though he was was not the only travelling Christian preacher in his day.

Our debt to Paul is, however, immense. The survival of some of his correspondence gives us the earliest material in the New Testament and shows us how Christianity spread rapidly in at least part of the Empire. In tracing the origins of Christianity the part played by Paul's letters is disproportionate to their length. Had it not been for Paul's work and his letters any investigation into Christian beginnings would be the poorer.

Texts

The second half of Acts and the Pauline letters are obviously relevant, and are referred to above. The following passages are of special importance: II Corinthians 10–13; Galatians 1–2; Philippians 3; Acts 9; 11.19–30.

Bibliography

G. Bornkamm, *Paul*, Hodder and Stoughton 1971; E. W. Hunt, *Portrait of Paul*, Mowbray 1968; Robert Jewitt, *Dating Paul's Life*, SCM Press 1979; D. E. H. Whiteley, *The Theology of St Paul*, Blackwell 1964.